八白土星命

Eight White Life Star

Feng Shui Essentials: Xuan Kong Nine Life Star
EIGHT WHITE LIFE STAR

Copyright © 2011 by Joey Yap
All rights reserved worldwide.
First Edition July 2011

All intellectual property rights contained or in relation to this book belongs to Joey Yap.

No part of this book may be copied, used, subsumed, or exploited in fact, field of thought or general idea, by any other authors or persons, or be stored in a retrieval system, transmitted or reproduced in any way, including but not limited to digital copying and printing in any form whatsoever worldwide without the prior agreement and written permission of the author.

The author can be reached at:

Mastery Academy of Chinese Metaphysics Sdn. Bhd. (611143-A)
19-3, The Boulevard, Mid Valley City,
59200 Kuala Lumpur, Malaysia.
Tel   : +603-2284 8080
Fax   : +603-2284 1218
Website : www.masteryacademy.com

DISCLAIMER:

The author, Joey Yap and the publisher, JY Books Sdn Bhd, have made their best efforts to produce this high quality, informative and helpful book. They have verified the technical accuracy of the information and contents of this book. Any information pertaining to the events, occurrences, dates and other details relating to the person or persons, dead or alive, and to the companies have been verified to the best of their abilities based on information obtained or extracted from various websites, newspaper clippings and other public media. However, they make no representation or warranties of any kind with regard to the contents of this book and accept no liability of any kind for any losses or damages caused or alleged to be caused directly or indirectly from using the information contained herein.

Published by JY Books Sdn. Bhd. (659134-T)

Table of content :

1	**LIFE STAR REFERENCE TABLE**	7
2	**INTRODUCTION**	12
3	**YOUR XUAN KONG LIFE STAR**	23
	Basic Attributes	24
4	**YOUR FENG SHUI ESSENTIALS**	27
	Directions	29
	Taking the Direction using a Compass	33
	Favorable Directions	39
	Unfavorable Directions	49
	Bed Alignment Direction	58
	Best Floor	60
	Personal Grand Duke Direction	65
	Personal Clash Direction	71
	Flying Star Effects	76
5	**THE FIVE ELEMENT**	97

6	**CHARACTERISTICS OF STAR**	109
	The Good	111
	The Bad	117
7	**CAREER AND WEALTH**	123
	Characteristics at work	124
	Suitable Job Roles	128
	Career and Wealth Guide	132
8	**RELATIONSHIPS**	139
	Guide for Relationships	140
9	**HEALTH**	145
	Guide for Health	146
10	**COMPATIBILITY with OTHER LIFE STARS**	151

LIFE STAR REFERENCE TABLE

Year Pillar and Gua Number Reference Table for 1912 - 2055

Animal	Year of Birth			Gua Number for Male	Gua Number for Female	Year of Birth			Gua Number for Male	Gua Number for Female
Rat	1912	壬子 Ren Zi	Water Rat	7	8	1936	丙子 Bing Zi	Fire Rat	1	5
Ox	1913	癸丑 Gui Chou	Water Ox	6	9	1937	丁丑 Ding Chou	Fire Ox	9	6
Tiger	1914	甲寅 Jia Yin	Wood Tiger	5	1	1938	戊寅 Wu Yin	Earth Tiger	8	7
Rabbit	1915	乙卯 Yi Mao	Wood Rabbit	4	2	1939	己卯 Ji Mao	Earth Rabbit	7	8
Dragon	1916	丙辰 Bing Chen	Fire Dragon	3	3	1940	庚辰 Geng Chen	Metal Dragon	6	9
Snake	1917	丁巳 Ding Si	Fire Snake	2	4	1941	辛巳 Xin Si	Metal Snake	5	1
Horse	1918	戊午 Wu Wu	Earth Horse	1	5	1942	壬午 Ren Wu	Water Horse	4	2
Goat	1919	己未 Ji Wei	Earth Goat	9	6	1943	癸未 Gui Wei	Water Goat	3	3
Monkey	1920	庚申 Geng Shen	Metal Monkey	8	7	1944	甲申 Jia Shen	Wood Monkey	2	4
Rooster	1921	辛酉 Xin You	Metal Rooster	7	8	1945	乙酉 Yi You	Wood Rooster	1	5
Dog	1922	壬戌 Ren Xu	Water Dog	6	9	1946	丙戌 Bing Xu	Fire Dog	9	6
Pig	1923	癸亥 Gui Hai	Water Pig	5	1	1947	丁亥 Ding Hai	Fire Pig	8	7
Rat	1924	甲子 Jia Zi	Wood Rat	4	2	1948	戊子 Wu Zi	Earth Rat	7	8
Ox	1925	乙丑 Yi Chou	Wood Ox	3	3	1949	己丑 Ji Chou	Earth Ox	6	9
Tiger	1926	丙寅 Bing Yin	Fire Tiger	2	4	1950	庚寅 Geng Yin	Metal Tiger	5	1
Rabbit	1927	丁卯 Ding Mao	Fire Rabbit	1	5	1951	辛卯 Xin Mao	Metal Rabbit	4	2
Dragon	1928	戊辰 Wu Chen	Earth Dragon	9	6	1952	壬辰 Ren Chen	Water Dragon	3	3
Snake	1929	己巳 Ji Si	Earth Snake	8	7	1953	癸巳 Gui Si	Water Snake	2	4
Horse	1930	庚午 Geng Wu	Metal Horse	7	8	1954	甲午 Jia Wu	Wood Horse	1	5
Goat	1931	辛未 Xin Wei	Metal Goat	6	9	1955	乙未 Yi Wei	Wood Goat	9	6
Monkey	1932	壬申 Ren Shen	Water Monkey	5	1	1956	丙申 Bing Shen	Fire Monkey	8	7
Rooster	1933	癸酉 Gui You	Water Rooster	4	2	1957	丁酉 Ding You	Fire Rooster	7	8
Dog	1934	甲戌 Jia Xu	Wood Dog	3	3	1958	戊戌 Wu Xu	Earth Dog	6	9
Pig	1935	乙亥 Yi Hai	Wood Pig	2	4	1959	己亥 Ji Hai	Earth Pig	5	1

- Please note that the date for the Chinese Solar Year starts on Feb 4. This means that if you were born in Feb 2 of 2002, you belong to the previous year 2001.

Year Pillar and Gua Number Reference Table for 1912 - 2055

Animal	Year of Birth			Gua Number for Male	Gua Number for Female	Year of Birth			Gua Number for Male	Gua Number for Female
Rat	1960	庚子 Geng Zi	Metal Rat	4	2	1984	甲子 Jia Zi	Wood Rat	7	8
Ox	1961	辛丑 Xin Chou	Metal Ox	3	3	1985	乙丑 Yi Chou	Wood Ox	6	9
Tiger	1962	壬寅 Ren Yin	Water Tiger	2	4	1986	丙寅 Bing Yin	Fire Tiger	5	1
Rabbit	1963	癸卯 Gui Mao	Water Rabbit	1	5	1987	丁卯 Ding Mao	Fire Rabbit	4	2
Dragon	1964	甲辰 Jia Chen	Wood Dragon	9	6	1988	戊辰 Wu Chen	Earth Dragon	3	3
Snake	1965	乙巳 Yi Si	Wood Snake	8	7	1989	己巳 Ji Si	Earth Snake	2	4
Horse	1966	丙午 Bing Wu	Fire Horse	7	8	1990	庚午 Geng Wu	Metal Horse	1	5
Goat	1967	丁未 Ding Wei	Fire Goat	6	9	1991	辛未 Xin Wei	Metal Goat	9	6
Monkey	1968	戊申 Wu Shen	Earth Monkey	5	1	1992	壬申 Ren Shen	Water Monkey	8	7
Rooster	1969	己酉 Ji You	Earth Rooster	4	2	1993	癸酉 Gui You	Water Rooster	7	8
Dog	1970	庚戌 Geng Xu	Metal Dog	3	3	1994	甲戌 Jia Xu	Wood Dog	6	9
Pig	1971	辛亥 Xin Hai	Metal Pig	2	4	1995	乙亥 Yi Hai	Wood Pig	5	1
Rat	1972	壬子 Ren Zi	Water Rat	1	5	1996	丙子 Bing Zi	Fire Rat	4	2
Ox	1973	癸丑 Gui Chou	Water Ox	9	6	1997	丁丑 Ding Chou	Fire Ox	3	3
Tiger	1974	甲寅 Jia Yin	Wood Tiger	8	7	1998	戊寅 Wu Yin	Earth Tiger	2	4
Rabbit	1975	乙卯 Yi Mao	Wood Rabbit	7	8	1999	己卯 Ji Mao	Earth Rabbit	1	5
Dragon	1976	丙辰 Bing Chen	Fire Dragon	6	9	2000	庚辰 Geng Chen	Metal Dragon	9	6
Snake	1977	丁巳 Ding Si	Fire Snake	5	1	2001	辛巳 Xin Si	Metal Snake	8	7
Horse	1978	戊午 Wu Wu	Earth Horse	4	2	2002	壬午 Ren Wu	Water Horse	7	8
Goat	1979	己未 Ji Wei	Earth Goat	3	3	2003	癸未 Gui Wei	Water Goat	6	9
Monkey	1980	庚申 Geng Shen	Metal Monkey	2	4	2004	甲申 Jia Shen	Wood Monkey	5	1
Rooster	1981	辛酉 Xin You	Metal Rooster	1	5	2005	乙酉 Yi You	Wood Rooster	4	2
Dog	1982	壬戌 Ren Xu	Water Dog	9	6	2006	丙戌 Bing Xu	Fire Dog	3	3
Pig	1983	癸亥 Gui Hai	Water Pig	8	7	2007	丁亥 Ding Hai	Fire Pig	2	4

- Please note that the date for the Chinese Solar Year starts on Feb 4. This means that if you were born in Feb 2 of 2002, you belong to the previous year 2001.

玄空九星命

Year Pillar and Gua Number Reference Table for 1912 - 2055

Animal	Year of Birth			Gua Number for		Year of Birth			Gua Number for	
				Male	Female				Male	Female
Rat	2008	戊子 Wu Zi	Earth Rat	1	5	2032	壬子 Ren Zi	Water Rat	4	2
Ox	2009	己丑 Ji Chou	Earth Ox	9	6	2033	癸丑 Gui Chou	Water Ox	3	3
Tiger	2010	庚寅 Geng Yin	Metal Tiger	8	7	2034	甲寅 Jia Yin	Wood Tiger	2	4
Rabbit	2011	辛卯 Xin Mao	Metal Rabbit	7	8	2035	乙卯 Yi Mao	Wood Rabbit	1	5
Dragon	2012	壬辰 Ren Chen	Water Dragon	6	9	2036	丙辰 Bing Chen	Fire Dragon	9	6
Snake	2013	癸巳 Gui Si	Water Snake	5	1	2037	丁巳 Ding Si	Fire Snake	8	7
Horse	2014	甲午 Jia Wu	Wood Horse	4	2	2038	戊午 Wu Wu	Earth Horse	7	8
Goat	2015	乙未 Yi Wei	Wood Goat	3	3	2039	己未 Ji Wei	Earth Goat	6	9
Monkey	2016	丙申 Bing Shen	Fire Monkey	2	4	2040	庚申 Geng Shen	Metal Monkey	5	1
Rooster	2017	丁酉 Ding You	Fire Rooster	1	5	2041	辛酉 Xin You	Metal Rooster	4	2
Dog	2018	戊戌 Wu Xu	Earth Dog	9	6	2042	壬戌 Ren Xu	Water Dog	3	3
Pig	2019	己亥 Ji Hai	Earth Pig	8	7	2043	癸亥 Gui Hai	Water Pig	2	4
Rat	2020	庚子 Geng Zi	Metal Rat	7	8	2044	甲子 Jia Zi	Wood Rat	1	5
Ox	2021	辛丑 Xin Chou	Metal Ox	6	9	2045	乙丑 Yi Chou	Wood Ox	9	6
Tiger	2022	壬寅 Ren Yin	Water Tiger	5	1	2046	丙寅 Bing Yin	Fire Tiger	8	7
Rabbit	2023	癸卯 Gui Mao	Water Rabbit	4	2	2047	丁卯 Ding Mao	Fire Rabbit	7	8
Dragon	2024	甲辰 Jia Chen	Wood Dragon	3	3	2048	戊辰 Wu Chen	Earth Dragon	6	9
Snake	2025	乙巳 Yi Si	Wood Snake	2	4	2049	己巳 Ji Si	Earth Snake	5	1
Horse	2026	丙午 Bing Wu	Fire Horse	1	5	2050	庚午 Geng Wu	Metal Horse	4	2
Goat	2027	丁未 Ding Wei	Fire Goat	9	6	2051	辛未 Xin Wei	Metal Goat	3	3
Monkey	2028	戊申 Wu Shen	Earth Monkey	8	7	2052	壬申 Ren Shen	Water Monkey	2	4
Rooster	2029	己酉 Ji You	Earth Rooster	7	8	2053	癸酉 Gui You	Water Rooster	1	5
Dog	2030	庚戌 Geng Xu	Metal Dog	6	9	2054	甲戌 Jia Xu	Wood Dog	9	6
Pig	2031	辛亥 Xin Hai	Metal Pig	5	1	2055	乙亥 Yi Hai	Wood Pig	8	7

- Please note that the date for the Chinese Solar Year starts on Feb 4. This means that if you were born in Feb 2 of 2002, you belong to the previous year 2001.

To download your Eight White Life Star Reference Chart FREE go to

www.masteryacademy.com/regbook

Here is your unique code for access:

GBSN6018

Introduction

When all is said and done, Feng Shui is the study of how environments affect the people living within them. It can yield advice on which environments, at both a macro and micro level, are 'good' places or 'bad' places to live for given people at given times.

Xuan Kong is only one subsection of the study of Feng Shui and the Life Stars are only one component in the Xuan Kong Feng Shui system. This means that the study of Life Stars gives us only one piece of the overall Feng Shui puzzle but it is an important one!

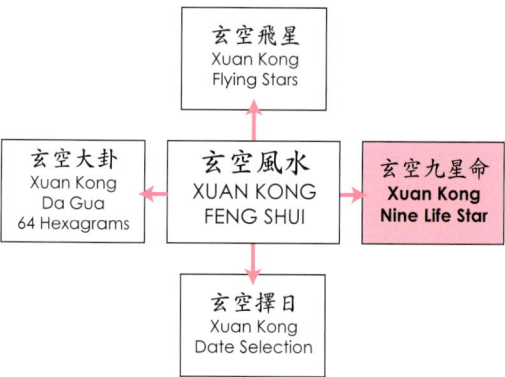

We can use the Xuan Kong Life Star system to help us with a number of practical Feng Shui and interpersonal decisions that make a big impact.

When we assess Feng Shui, we assess four factors: Environment, Buildings, Time and People. This book has been written to complement a number of other Feng Shui titles;

1. *Feng Shui for Homebuyers – Exterior;*
2. *Feng Shui for Homebuyers – Interior;*
3. *Feng Shui for Apartment Buyers;* and
4. *Pure Feng Shui.*

These other books talk about the influence of Environment, Buildings and Time on Feng Shui. This book looks at the final aspect: **People.**

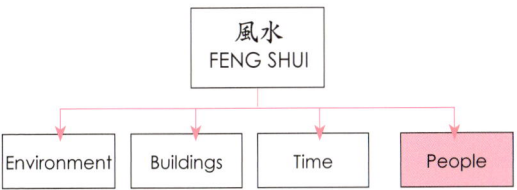

Different people will be affected in different ways by any given environment. The Life Stars directly determine what role the environment plays in the lives of its occupants. Every person is governed by one of the 9 Life Stars. These Stars also help determine key personal characteristics.

In this book, you will learn how the annually changing Xuan Kong Flying Stars interact with your Life Star so that you know what different sectors of your home will bring you. You can then use this information for your own benefit and safety. For maximum benefit, people should seek to align themselves with the direction in their home that yields positive effects. For instance, the #9 Purple Flying Star brings about the potential of career advancement for Star 1 people. Clearly this is a benefit that professionally minded people would like to take advantage of, so they may wish to spend more time absorbing the influence of the #9 Purple Flying Star in their home or place of work. The same Flying Star also indicates a heightened risk of miscarriage for pregnant women though and so pregnant Life Star 1 women should be exercise heightened caution in the presence of this Flying Star, and avoid its influence if possible.

Because the advice generated by this book on Xuan Kong Life Stars takes into account your Life Star when discussing the effects of the Flying Stars, the advice given is highly tailored to your life.

The Positive Side Of You

Your Life Star brings a force to bear on you, wherever you are. This force can have positive or negative effects, depending on the Feng Shui of the environment you reside in.

We are all multi faceted and complex. We have good habits and bad habits; a strong side and a weak side. By correctly tapping into the right Qi your best side will manifest itself more. When you put your best foot forward more in life, more opportunities

and success comes your way. Conversely, if you find yourself under the negative influence of your Life Star, more of your negative personality traits will prevail. Your environment filters out the good or the bad influence of your Life Star. Xuan Kong Feng Shui shows us how we can align ourself to receive the best possible influence. By simply aligning your bed and study desk to correspond with your favourable Personal Directions for example, you can already take one big step towards absorbing the beneficial influence of your Life Star, even whilst you sleep and study! If you are choosing a new home then choosing the correct floor at the correct time will bring further benefits. Avoiding your Personal Grand Duke and Crash Sectors will keep health problems and conflict at bay.

Does all of this mean you must tip-toe around certain rooms in your house or seal them off? No. Feng Shui does not need to become all consuming. If you can easily align your bed so that you receive benefits then why not do so? There are real world limits to what can be done, it is not practical, for instance, to rebuild your home if it does not perfectly cater to the instructions that this book gives. Your ideal floor choice in a condominium may not be available. The list of real world complications goes on.

You can tailor Feng Shui to work for you; making smaller, simple changes so that you reap the maximum possible benefit. The pursuit of good Feng Shui is not intended to take up all of your time and this flexible book is perfect for anyone, no matter how busy or restricted you are in your decisions.

Your Life Star

Everyone falls under the jurisdiction of one of the 9 Life Stars and this will have different consequences for everyone. Your Life Star describes your key skills, characteristics and traits. Some people are creative but reserved, some people are aggressive and driven. What self destructive traits do you have? Do you have a bloated sense of pride or are you prone to gossip? Your Life Star can shine some light on the complexity of your personality and your good and bad traits.

Study of the Life Stars has practical benefits for everyone; it gives you valuable information about others in addition to yourself. Different Life Stars bestow different abilities on people which means that people belonging to each Star will exhibit different characteristics at work. A Star 1 person is diplomatic so they are best suited to roles demanding diplomacy, for example. Accordingly, employers can study the Xuan Kong Life Stars when making work place decisions whilst employees can use the system to help them go about working productively with their colleagues and superiors, even when disagreements arise.

If you become aware of your own harmful tendencies then you can learn to minimize them so you can advance. Similar benefits can be seen in romantic relationships and friendships. Learning that a Star 7 individual needs their space and independence

might help you accommodate this in your dealings with them when you might otherwise have been tempted to be clingy and dependant.

When we understand more about ourselves we can stop ourselves from making mistakes and perhaps forgive certain behaviour in others once we understand where it comes from.

Compatibility Guide

Certain people are, of course, more compatible with each other than others. In partnerships or relationships this takes on a new level of importance. Different Life Stars bestow the qualities of different elements on different people; for example, a Star 1 person has the qualities of water whilst a Star 7 person has the qualities of the Yin Metal element. Just as the elements control, pacify and weaken one another, individuals of the different Stars may dominate, clash with or enrich one another. This book includes a write up of how compatible different Stars are with one another. You may find that a relationship as a Star 1 person with a Star 5 person simply isn't worth the effort. A compatibility guide on each interaction gives you tips on how to best deal with the other Stars for mutual benefit, even taking into account your differences.

Compatible With BaZi Profiling Systems

If you are familiar with the **BaZi Profiling System** then you will be aware that, at first glance, it seems to deal with very similar issues. It can tell us about other preferences and internal view of the world. Do we have an optimistic view of things? Do we blame ourselves too much?

While there is some overlap between the jurisdiction of the Xuan Kong Life Star system and BaZi Profiling System, they are two different systems. They both deal with individual people and their personalities but they are not mutually exclusive. In fact, when studied together, they can be thought of as two pieces of the same puzzle.

The BaZi Profiling System tells us about ourselves and about others. It even tells us things that cannot be observed about others (things people do not communicate). What it can't tell us is how the outside environment plays into the picture. The Xuan Kong Nine Stars help determine *which* qualities are brought out and by what features and external forms in the environment.

Once we know what directions are conducive to good Qi, how external forms (pylons etc) can compound problems related to sectors in the home, which areas of our environment increase the risk of which ailments or even which people can create problems in our lives (compatibility guide) then we can begin shaping our external environment to whatever degree necessary in order to enjoy the most happiness, wealth and success. Xuan

Kong Feng Shui tells you precisely what effect the environment and compass directions will have on which people.

If you are simply interested in learning what makes a person tick rather than making decisions about an ideal environment for them to thrive in then I recommend you take up further study of the BaZi Profiling System. The goal of BaZi is to pinpoint personal deficiencies so that they may be overcome or to highlight personal strengths so that they may be capitalised on.

If you are trying to configure your environment in order to maximize the benefits that your home or place of work bestow upon you in terms of health, wealth and relationships, then the Feng Shui Xuan Kong Life Star system is the one for you.

When you combine the two systems and employ them on yourself you will be able to make the most of your best qualities and then seek out an environment which lets you shine and gives the least resistance. A powerful combination of self improvement and informed decision making!

An Easier Life

Life doesn't have to be difficult. It is possible to effectively dodge conflict, problem situations and health problems if you know they are coming. The Life Stars hold the key to many of the "surprises" that life has in store for us and we can learn to shape our environment to our own advantage. This is exciting stuff! Seeking out the best romantic relationships and business opportunities is a top priority for most people and the power of your Life Star can be called upon in these pursuits.

Even though much is made of the layout of the home with relation to Feng Shui, you won't need to bend over backwards to accommodate the advice given in this book. For instance, where you cannot choose the ideal living floor specified, second and third choices are mentioned. You can take as much or as little from this book as you need without fear of it making you paranoid and prey to "paralysis by analysis". Looking back on your own life, you can most probably think of two or three big mistakes – a bad business deal or choice in romantic partner, perhaps. Avoiding pitfalls of this magnitude in the future is made a whole lot easier when you have some idea of how likely they are to occur. If you can make changes to your environment to further reduce this likelihood then all the better!

I hope that this book expands your world view. Once you know how to utilize them, the Nine Stars can be the harbinger of great fortune instead of misery for you. If you can stay on the 'correct side' of your Star and always position yourself to bask in its positive influence then many happy successes await you.

Joey Yap
July, 2011

 www.facebook.com/joeyyapFB

Author's personal website :
www.joeyyap.com

Academy websites :
www.masteryacademy.com | www.maelearning.com | www.baziprofiling.com

八白土星命
Eight White Life Star

Life Star 8	Born in
Male	1929, 1938, 1947, 1956, 1965, 1974, 1983, 1992, 2001, 2010
Female	1921, 1930, 1939, 1948, 1957, 1966, 1975, 1984, 1993, 2002

• Please note that the date for the Chinese Solar Year starts on Feb 4. This means that if you were born in Feb 2 of 2002, you belong to the previous year 2001.

Your Xuan Kong Life Star

Your Xuan Kong Life Star is Gua #8, and your trigram is called Gen. It looks like this:

For the rest of this book, we will refer to your Gua #8 as Life Star 8.

Basic Attributes of Star 8

Your Life Star 8 is of the Yang Earth element, and as such it shares some of the traits of Earth when it its Yang qualities manifest themselves. Yang Earth is associated with big immovable rock formations and mountains, and accordingly it represents solidity, calmness, and a certain form of majesty.

As a Life Star 8, you are known to possess the characteristics of dependability and solidity. Just like the mountain, you are someone who is always present and seldom changing. You exude an aura of calm and certainty. Once you make up your mind about something, you will rarely change your it. This does not mean that you create conflict, however, as you do not seek out arguments with others and when they do arise you do not adopt an abrasive approach. In your own quiet way, you will decide on something and stick to it.

Your outward exterior of cool, collected placidity can hide a depth of feeling and opinion which you hold inside. Sometimes, however, you can lose the ability to express your feelings and thoughts to others because you've become so used to hiding them and presenting a helpful,

reliable exterior to everyone else. As such, you may face problems articulating your feelings when the right time comes along. You can also be rigid and stubborn and utterly resistant to change if you don't like it, and because you like to think things through you sometimes don't realize when you're reacting too slowly, missing out on important events.

Basic Emotions & Temperament

Plus : Reliable, consistent, striving, persistent, energetic

Minus: Suspicious, opinionated, stagnated, possessive, self-indulgent

YOUR FENG SHUI ESSENTIALS

The Feng Shui Essentials comprise Feng Shui Directions, the effects of the Xuan Kong Nine Stars in various sectors and areas of your home and workspace, and the Five Elements.

Each of these factors interact with your Life Star in different ways that will affect how your Life Star manifests itself and determine whether or not it brings out good or bad qualities in you.

方向

Directions

Directions

Direction is an integral component of understanding Xuan Kong Nine Life Stars. Different directions in your home and your place of work can either accentuate or depreciate the strength of your Life Star.

Favorable Direction will highlight or enhance the positive traits of your Life Star, while an Unfavorable Direction will diminish or weaken your Life Star and bring out some of its negative attributes.

The Life Star numbers are categorized into two groups: the East Group and the West Group. The names 'East Group' and 'West Group' are just to demarcate the Greater and Lesser Yin transformation of the Tai Ji. They do not literally represent directions.

East Group Life Stars include 1, 3, 4 and 9. Those who are Life Stars 2, 6, 7 and 8 belong to the West Group. The following table will give you a quick reference of the Auspicious and Inauspicious compass directions of the East and West Group.

East Group 東命

卦 Gua	生氣 Shen Qi Life Generating	天醫 Tian Yi Heavenly Doctor	延年 Yan Nian Longevity	伏位 Fu Wei Stability	禍害 Huo Hai Mishaps	五鬼 Wu Gui Five Ghosts	六煞 Liu Sha Six Killings	絕命 Jue Ming Life Threatening
坎 Kan 1 Water	東南 South East	東 East	南 South	北 North	西 West	東北 North East	西北 North West	西南 South West
震 Zhen 3 Wood	南 South	北 North	東南 South East	東 East	西南 South West	西北 North West	東北 North East	西 West
巽 Xun 4 Wood	北 North	南 South	東 East	東南 South East	西北 North West	西南 South West	西 West	東北 North East
離 Li 9 Fire	東 East	東南 South East	北 North	南 South	東北 North East	西 West	西南 South West	西北 North West

West Group 西命

卦 Gua	生氣 Shen Qi Life Generating	天醫 Tian Yi Heavenly Doctor	延年 Yan Nian Longevity	伏位 Fu Wei Stability	禍害 Huo Hai Mishaps	五鬼 Wu Gui Five Ghosts	六煞 Liu Sha Six Killings	絕命 Jue Ming Life Threatening
坤 Kun 2 Earth	東北 North East	西 West	西北 North West	西南 South West	東 East	東南 South East	南 South	北 North
乾 Qian 6 Metal	西 West	東北 North East	西南 South West	西北 North West	東南 South East	東 East	北 North	南 South
兌 Dui 7 Metal	西北 North West	西南 South West	東北 North East	西 West	北 North	南 South	東南 South East	東 East
► 艮 Gen 8 Earth	西南 South West	西北 North West	西 West	東北 North East	南 South	北 North	東 East	東南 South East

The concepts of Favorable and Unfavorable are derived from the Eight Wandering Stars system of the Ba Zhai Eight Mansion Feng Shui 八宅風水.

Each of the 8 directions is governed by a Star. These Wandering Stars will affect each Xuan Kong Life Star in different ways. Each Life Star has four Favorable Directions governed by Auspicious Stars: Sheng Qi 生氣 (Life Generating), Tian Yi 天醫 (Heavenly Doctor), Yan Nian 延年 (Longevity), and Fu Wei 伏位 (Stability).

The four Unfavorable Directions are governed by Inauspicious Stars and include Huo Hai 禍害 (Mishaps), Wu Gui 五鬼 (Five Ghost), Liu Sha 六煞 (Six Killings) and Jue Ming 絕命 (Life Diminishing).

The following diagram shows you the Favorable and Unfavorable Directions for Star 8.

Taking the Direction using a Compass

You will need a compass – or alternatively, the Joey Yap iLuoPan app for iPhone available at the Apple App Store – to determine the direction of your Main Door, Bed and Stove. Hold your compass or iLuoPan at waist level as shown on the illustration below. Your compass or iLuoPan will align to the magnetic North on its own. All you need to know is how to take your direction as indicated on the following pages.

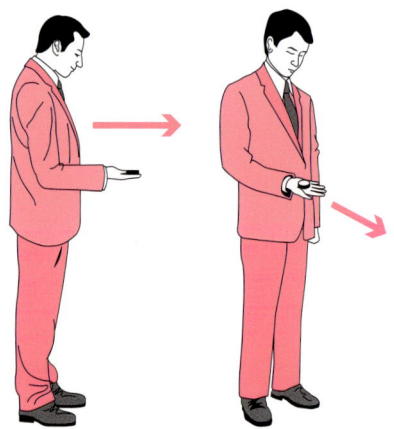

Facing Direction of the Main Door

1. Stand about one foot outside the door looking outwards.

2. Use the square base of your compass to help you align yourself parallel to the door.

3. Read the facing direction on your compass.

Facing Direction of the Bed

1. Measure from the head of the bed where your head is placed when you lie down (the direction the headboard faces) and not the direction your feet face.

Facing Direction of the Stove

1. For modern (gas or electric) stoves, look at the where direction of the cooking knobs (fire igniters) are pointing to determine its facing direction.

2. For traditional stoves that require wood and fire to work, look for their 'fire mouth' as the facing direction.

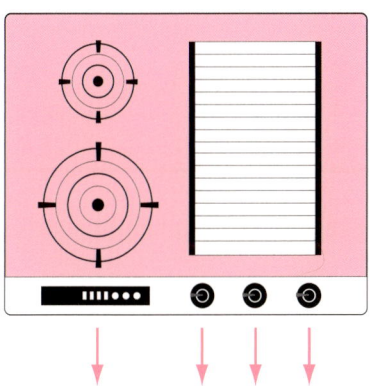

Favorable Directions

Southwest
西南 (217.6°-232.5°)

Life Generating
生氣 (Sheng Qi)

 **The basic characteristics of the Sheng Qi Star:**

It brings about promotions, career advancements, strong money and wealth luck, potential political power and authority, and all-round success.

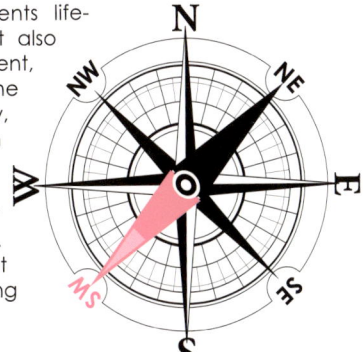

The Sheng Qi Star represents life-generating Qi or energy. It also represents the Wood Element, and hence, governs the facets of success, authority, nobility, status and wealth in life. Wood relates to growth and advancement in life, and as such is an extremely auspicious Star to tap into. For you, the Southwest direction taps into the Sheng Qi potential.

This Star is suitable for business (commercial), career and wealth-related pursuits. It would therefore be ideal for a business or residence to have its Main Door situated in the Sheng Qi sector as it allows you to tap into these energies to create opportunities for profit and long term wealth opportunities.

Sheng Qi is an active star by nature and thus, it is not conducive for rest or sleep-related activities. It is best to avoid having the bed or bedroom located in this sector or for anyone to sleep facing this direction. Use this sector for your work or for active pursuits instead of relaxing ones.

If this sector is missing from a house or is lacking in the office or the premises of a business, the wealth-related aspects of your career or venture will be considerably weakened and it will be a difficult struggle to amass wealth and prosperity.

Northwest
西北 (307.6°-322.5°)

Heavenly Doctor
天醫 *(Tian Yi)*

The basic characteristics of the Tian Yi Star:

It brings about general good luck and well-being, as well as positive mentor luck or the presence of sound advisors and guidance.

This Star represents the Earth Element and is therefore the determinant of noble people (mentors) and people of caliber and status. It also denotes your health prospects and physical wellbeing. As such, the Tian Yi Star is best utilized to help generate guidance for your career or for any project which you've embarked upon. It will bring about the help and assistance of others.

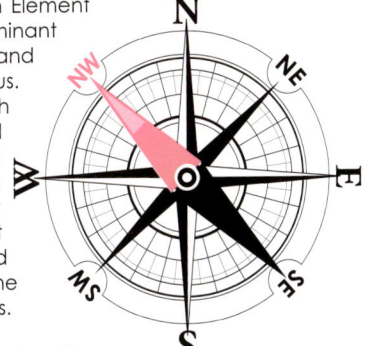

It is also a useful Star for health purposes, and its benefits can be employed when you need to recuperate, recover, or heal from an illness, surgical procedure or health issue.

When the Tian Yin sector is missing from a home or office, your health is likely to suffer because of it. In addition, you will also find help from noble people hard to come by, especially in times of need in life and career matters. You will come across more obstacles and obstructions which you must overcome on your own without the external help of others.

Since the Tian Yi Star represents nobility, it also governs your reputation, respectability, and your oratory powers. It thus has influence on your powers of speech and persuasion, and has some bearing on how you are perceived by others and how well they respond to your verbal overtures.

West
西 (262.6°-277.5°)

Longevity
延年 *(Yan Nian)*

The basic characteristics of the Yan Nian Star:

It prolongs and enhances life and improves the quality of your life. It promotes good communication with others which in turn makes for good relationships.

The Yan Nian Star represents the Metal Element, and as such governs speech and the effectiveness of your words. If you are looking to establish good relationships and rapport with others, you will need the help of this Star, since it governs aspects of successful networking, communication and relationship building.

The Yan Nian Star is important for family harmony and domestic bliss. It is also necessary if you wish to build good relationships with co-workers and colleagues. Essentially, it paves the way for smooth interpersonal relations, seldom plagued by misunderstanding, arguments and flare-ups. As such, the presence of the Yan Nian Star is useful for maintaining harmony.

If you are employed in public relations or marketing and you must interact with clients and customers as part of your daily routine, you will find the Qi brought about by this Star very useful to your career.

Do note that if the Yan Nian sector is missing, harmony and unity will be adversely affected, and relations are likely to be tense or strained. At the very least, you can expect more argument and discord with others.

Northeast
東北 (37.6°-52.5°)

Stability
伏位 (Fu Wei)

The basic characteristics of the Fu Wei Star:

It is a Star that promotes calm and keeps you grounded. It allows for peace of mind and rationality. It also promotes good luck.

The Fu Wei Star represents the Wood Element. When qualities or virtues such as calmness and tranquility are required, this is the Star you need! It promotes peace of mind and heightens clarity of thought, so this is also the Star to use if you need to focus, study or make important decisions.

If you wish to practice mediation or undertake religious and spiritual observances, the Fu Wei Star will provide the energies needed for calm and serenity, enhancing mental health and wellbeing.

This Star is most suitably applied to libraries, study areas/zones or other places where concentration is necessary. When considering the home or workplace, this Star can help create areas where the mind can be easily quietened and people can reflect and turn inward.

When the Fu Wei sector is missing from a place, peace of mind will be difficult to attain.

Unfavorable Directions

South
南 (172.6°-187.5°)

Mishaps
祸害 (Huo Hai)

The basic characteristics of the Huo Hai Star: It denotes potential calamities, accidents, and mishaps. It undermines good efforts, and brings about the risk of mistakes and errors.

The Huo Hai Star represents the Earth Element and is the harbinger of mishaps, loss of wealth, sudden (unfortunate) changes or hassles as well as work-related obstacles. What it does is undermine your efforts and bring about sudden obstructions or problems that will result in a loss of time and energy.

If, for example, the Main Door of a property is located in this direction, you can reasonably expect to encounter quite a few obstacles and problems in your daily life. It is best to work around this area particularly if your main door or office is located in the West sector.

The detrimental effects of a negative star are compounded when it is located within an area that is already affected by negative Feng Shui, so pay attention to the negative structures outside this area.

North
北 (352.6°-7.5°)

Five Ghosts
五鬼 *(Wu Gui)*

The basic characteristics of the Wu Gui Star:

It brings about betrayal and treachery through back-stabbing, gossip, and rumors. It also denotes endless bickering and fraught tension brought about by arguments.

The Wu Gui Star represents the Fire Element and is the bringer of betrayal, ill-intentioned gossip, rumours, backstabbing, cruelty, petty people and even subterfuge and sabotage. It generally denotes a sense of unease brought upon by less-than-honest speech.

The presence of Wu Gui in a house causes disloyalty and discord amongst family members, affecting relationships and marriages. If it is present in your work place, then you should also watch out for fights and arguments between your colleagues or subordinates and friction or tension with your superiors.

Negative external forms such as (sharp) pylons and jagged rooftops pointing towards a house further aggravate the effects of this Star.

East
東 (82.6°-97.5°)

Six Killings
六煞 (Liu Sha)

The basic characteristics of the Liu Sha Star:

This Star brings about injuries and accidents. It also denotes the possibility of betrayals and dishonesty, and the risk of potential scandals.

The Liu Sha Star relates to the element of Water and is the harbinger of lawsuits and potential scandals. Legal problems at the workplace or adulterous affairs in relation to your marriage or personal relationships could be brought to light.

This Star is also the harbinger of bodily injury, harm and conditions requiring people to undergo physical surgery. Robberies and theft are also likely, and you will have to be careful about what information you share with others and with the general safety of your personal documents and possessions.

Be mindful of the presence of negative external forms, which will compound the adverse effects of this Star. For instance, a Y-shaped road at the Liu Sha sector will result in scandalous affairs, while negative structures as mentioned earlier will compound and exacerbate the harmful effects of the Liu Sha Star.

Southeast
東南 (127.6°-142.5°)

Life Threatening
絕命 *(Jue Ming)*

The basic characteristics of the Jue Ming Star:

It brings about the risk of accidents and major illness, and the threat of miscarriage for pregnant women. It also signals potential for great calamity.

This Star represents the Metal Element and it signifies accidents and illnesses. The energies of the Jue Ming Star are quite severe and so are its adverse effects, bringing with it considerable risk.

In severe cases, the Jue Ming Star can even cause fatal accidents, ailments or injuries when there are negative external forms outside of the Southeast sector.

It is to no surprise that this star is often regarded as the primary star of misfortune and calamity in the study of Ba Zhai Feng Shui. Other than catastrophes and accidents, it can also cause major loss of wealth and theft as well as the cause of breakups or separation in relationships.

Bed Alignment Direction

One of the key Feng Shui factors of the bedroom is how your bed is placed. For starters, your bed should preferably be pushed against a wall, with the headboard also against it. The most important thing you can do when laying out your bedroom with regards to Feng Shui is to make sure your headboard is aligned with your Favorable Direction.

Facing Direction, in the case of bed alignment, refers to the direction of your headboard. This means it is the direction your head faces when you lie down on the bed, and **not** the direction that your feet face.

As a Star 8, your Bed Alignment Directions are:

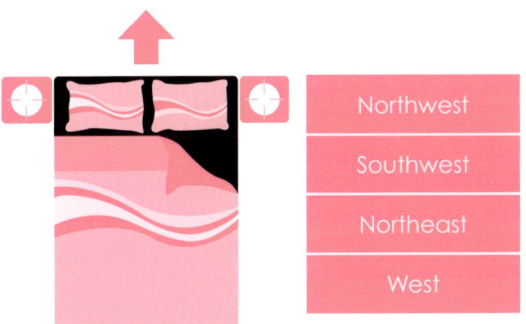

Best Floor

A reality of modern life is that most of us do not live in houses these days, instead living in multi story apartments and condominium blocks.

Some of us are pretty mobile and live a nomad-like lifestyle that may require us to stay in high-rise buildings for certain periods of time. As such, it becomes important to select the right floor to reside in. The objective of this is to achieve elemental affinity between you (the occupant) with the energies of a particular floor.

As you are a Star 8 person of the Earth element, the chart below gives you the best floors for you to live on in terms of first choice, second choice, and third choice.

First Choice	Second Choice	Third Choice
5th Floor	2nd Floor	1st Floor
10th Floor	7th Floor	6th Floor
15th Floor	12th Floor	11th Floor
20th Floor	17th Floor	16th Floor
25th Floor	22nd Floor	21th Floor
30th Floor	27th Floor	26th Floor
35th Floor	32th Floor	31th Floor
40th Floor	37th Floor	36th Floor
45th Floor	42th Floor	41st Floor
50th Floor	47th Floor	46th Floor

Select :
Fire shaped buildings & Earth shaped buildings

Avoid :
Wood shaped buildings & Metal shaped buildings

Personal Grand Duke Directions

Identifying the Grand Duke Sector is important. Your Personal Grand Duke Sector relates to your birth year. For example, if you are born in the year of the Rat then the Rat is your Personal Grand Duke and we know that the Rat sector is North 2.

We want to avoid the harmful properties of this area and as you are a Star 8 person, you can locate your Personal Grand Duke Sector in the following directions:

Personal Grand Duke Directions for Male

MALE Birth Year	Personal Grand Duke	Direction
1920, 1956, 1992, 2028	申 Shen Monkey	西南3 Southwest 3
1929, 1965, 2001, 2037	巳 Si Snake	東南3 Southeast 3
1938, 1974, 2010, 2046	寅 Yin Tiger	東北3 Northeast 3
1947, 1983, 2019, 2055	亥 Hai Pig	西北3 Northwest 3

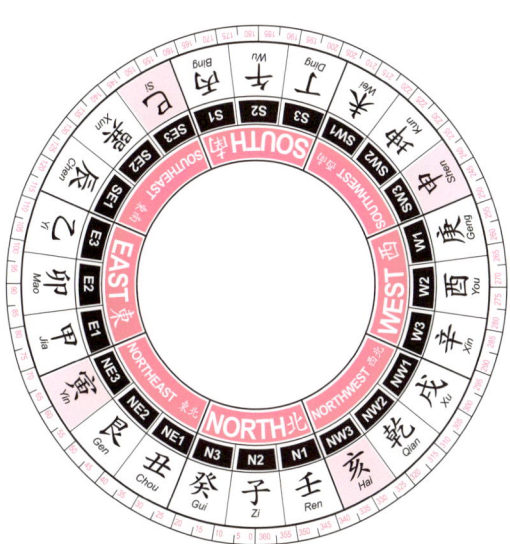

Personal Grand Duke Directions for Female

FEMALE Birth Year	Personal Grand Duke	Direction
1912, 1948, 1984, 2020	子 Zi Rat	北 2 **North 2**
1921, 1957, 1993, 2029	酉 You Rooster	西 2 **West 2**
1930, 1966, 2002, 2038	午 Wu Horse	南 2 **South 2**
1939, 1975, 2011, 2047	卯 Mao Rabbit	東 2 **East 2**

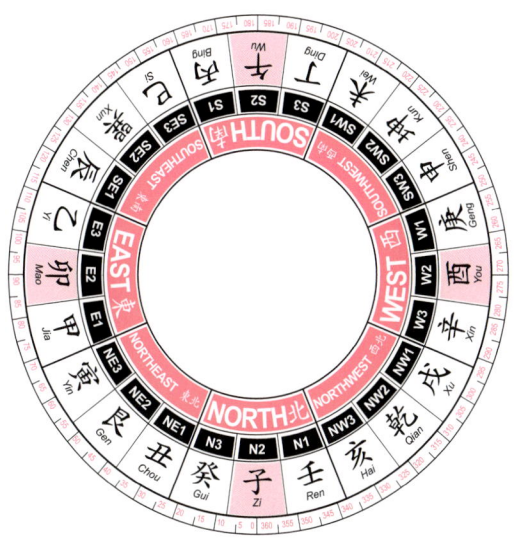

Ideally, you should not have a bathroom or toilet located in these areas of your home above and Sha Qi external features such as pylons, T-junctions, Dead Tree should be avoided. The Sha Qi in the Personal Grand Duke Sector is extremely strong and so all efforts to avoid spending a lot of time in it should be made. It goes without saying that the Personal Grand Duke Sector of your home is not the ideal spot for a bedroom! The Sha Qi in this area of the home is so strong in fact that it is difficult for any further negative Qi to enter!

煞方

Personal Clash Directions

Your home will contain Personal Clash Sectors. Spending time in these areas of your home will bring up problems in your life with significant others. As a Star 8 person, you will find your Personal Clash Sectors in the following directions:

Personal Clash Directions for Male

MALE Birth Year	Personal Clash Sector	Direction
1920, 1956, 1992, 2028	寅 *Yin* **Tiger**	東北 3 **Northeast 3**
1929, 1965, 2001, 2037	亥 *Hai* **Pig**	西北 3 **Northwest 3**
1938, 1974, 2010, 2046	申 *Shen* **Monkey**	西南 3 **Southwest 3**
1947, 1983, 2019, 2055	巳 *Si* **Snake**	東南 3 **Southeast 3**

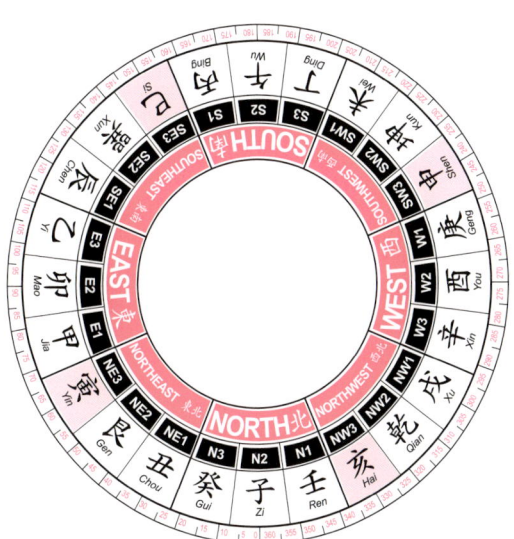

Personal Clash Directions for Female

FEMALE Birth Year	Personal Grand Duke	Direction
1912, 1948, 1984, 2020	午 Wu Horse	南 2 South 2
1921, 1957, 1993, 2029	卯 Mao Rabbit	東 2 East 2
1930, 1966, 2002, 2038	子 Zi Rat	北 2 North 2
1939, 1975, 2011, 2047	酉 You Rooster	西 2 West 2

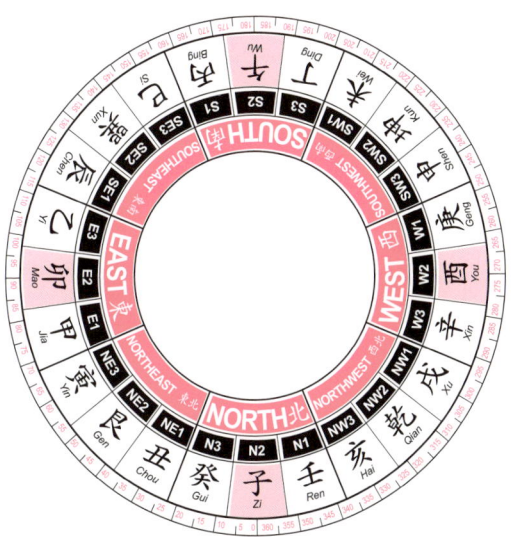

The locations above are a bad place for important features of your home such as the main door, bedroom and kitchen. You should seek to avoid these sectors in the same way you avoid your Personal Grand Duke Sector.

Flying Stars Effects

Each year, the Xuan Kong Flying Stars fly into a different section of a property, be it your residence or your work space. The effects that these Nine Stars have on you will be different depending on your Life Star. In this section you can find out how different Flying Stars in different sectors will effect you with regards to Feng Shui.

The Flying Stars have both negative and positive attributes, but which facets will show when you see a particular Star, depends on the timeliness and the period.

A few of the Nine Stars are inherently negative, a few are inherently positive in nature and some can be both good and bad. Even then, we must remember that the Stars have the capacity to manifest either their positive or negative facets because in Feng Shui, nothing is ever inherently bad or good forever.

When it comes to Flying Stars, it is important to remember this key principle: Forms activate the Stars and the Stars in turn influence the People. This is what you should keep in mind as you read about the effects of the Nine Stars on your Life Star.

1 ★ → 8 White Life

The effects of the visiting #1 White Star on a 8 White Life:

In terms of Feng Shui effects, the presence of the #1 White Star is somewhat less than auspicious for older men of the Star 8 who are using this sector. It can induce some health problems, most likely bladder illness or infections. Young Star 8 children may also have to deal with ear infections. In the presence of positive external Feng Shui arrangement, however, the #1 White brings good news in the form of wealth luck. You are likely to enjoy a sudden beneficial windfall or perhaps even gain a salary increase. When its positive influence is felt and harnessed, # 1 White can also result in academically-gifted children.

2★ → 8 White Life

The effects of the visiting **#2 Black Star** on a **8 White Life:**

In terms of Feng Shui effects, the presence of the #2 Black can be the harbinger of certain gastrointestinal health problems. You may find yourself having to visit the doctor more frequently, and you may have to change or adjust your diet to find relief from your symptoms. #2 Black can also bring about wealth loss and potential financial devastation, although if there are positive external factors the #2 Black can boost your reputation and stature and allow you to enjoy greater respect and authority at your workplace.

3★ → 8 White Life

The effects of the visiting #3 Jade Star on a 8 White Life:

In terms of Feng Shui effects, the #3 Jade will not be beneficial for Star 8 children, particularly those under the age of 12. They may find themselves having to deal with emotional problems, and may have to battle discontent and feelings of rebellion. Problems may crop up with their peers at school. On the other hand, when boosted by positive external factors, the #3 Jade can bring increased authority for the Star 8 adult. If you are in a position of leadership at the workplace and need to unite a group of people together to move forward in a project, the energy of this Star will help consolidate your authority and make sure that people heed your instructions, generating results.

4★ → 8 White Life

The effects of the visiting **#4 Green Star** on a **8 White Life**:

In terms of Feng Shui effects, the presence of the #4 Green also brings about the possibility of illness. Kidney problems are particularity likely. When the influence of #4 Green is present you will have to contend with. If you are married or newly-wed, the #4 Green will not exactly bestow bliss or forthcoming intimacy. On the contrary, the energy of the Star may contribute towards marital discord and create a sense of distance. You will find yourself and your partner at each others throats more often than usual as fights and arguments break out between you.

5★ → 8 White Life

The effects of the visiting #5 Yellow Star on a 8 White Life:

In terms of Feng Shui effects, the presence of the #5 Yellow can bring about financial success and lucrative opportunities. You will enjoy an increase in your income and you may even gain a secondary income. However, whether or not this comes to pass depends on whether the external Feng Shui factors are positive. If there are negative features (sharp pylons located outside this sector, for example), then the reverse will be true for your wealth luck, and financial loss becomes a risk. Furthermore, the #5 Yellow is quite dangerous in that it brings about the possibility of illness that in some very extreme cases can prove fatal. Some of the extreme manifestations of it include cancer and paralysis.

6★ → 8 White Life

The effects of the visiting **#6 White Star** on a **8 White Life**:

In terms of Feng Shui effects, the presence of the #6 White is actually very good for the Star 8 person and is generally regarded as auspicious. This is because the #6 White is as benevolent as the Star 8 person, and this makes for a winning combination! Get ready to make progress in your life. At work, you can expect #6 White to facilitate renewed career progress. You might be offered a new job or simply some form of promotion. The presence of the #6 White will also bring about a boost in your reputation and you will receive more respect from others for the work that you do. You may even gain some measure of fame as a result.

7★ → 8 White Life

The effects of the visiting **#7 Red Star** on a **8 White Life**:

In terms of Feng Shui effects, the presence of the #7 Red bodes well for your financial luck. Where money is concerned, the potential for windfall gains are likely, so you must be quick on your feet if you are to capitalizing on timely financial opportunities. This is especially true if you wish to acquire a secondary income or make good use of indirect wealth luck. The #7 Red also bodes well for your romantic endeavors. Where romance is concerned, you can also use the good energies of the #8 White to meet more people and embark on a relationship if you're single. The likelihood of meeting a suitable partner is high.

8★ → 8 White Life

The effects of the visiting **#8 White Star** on a **8 White Life:**

In terms of Feng Shui effects, the presence of the #8 White can be a mixed blessing, although it can yield some very positive results if its influence is channelled correctly by positive external Feng Shui factors. Primarily, it can provide boost to your financial state if you know how to best make the most of the opportunities that come your way. That's because the opportunities for increased wealth luck may not be so obvious in terms of a direct salary boost. You may have to get creative with extra income possibilities, or possibly see if you can do something with your talents on the side to generate profitable results. You must make the effort if you want to make the gains this #8 White facilitates.

9 ★ → 8 White Life

The effects of the visiting **#9 Purple Star** on a **8 White Life:**

In terms of Feng Shui effects, the presence of the #9 Purple means many happy developments lie ahead for you, and as such this is a welcome star. Joyous events tend to take place with the help of the #9 Purple, and its energy will also improve your mood. You will find yourself feeling more optimistic with the presence of this Star. In your career, look forward to a period of plain sailing. Nothing will stand in your path and you should prepare for and some welcome news involving career advancement or a possible promotion. For those of you in relationships, there is likely to be good news in the form of a proposal or marriage plans! All in all, #9 Purple is great for Star 8 individuals.

五行

THE FIVE ELEMENTS

The Five Elements

The element of your Life Star 8 is (Yang) Earth, and it is important that you understand the implications of this. In the study of Chinese Metaphysics and Feng Shui, a basic understanding of the Five Elements is integral to success. This section will briefly outline the role of the Five Elements.

The Five Elements are symbolic representations of energy, or Qi. In Feng Shui and in BaZi, the Five Elements are Earth, Metal, Water, Wood, and Fire. Earth represents stability and trust, and Yang Earth which is associated with large rocks and mountains denotes solidity, dignity, and a noble nature.

In order to understand the elements, it's important to understand their relationship to one another. Each element does not exist in isolation. As such, these elements share three important relationships known as 'cycles' that are fundamental to the understanding of Feng Shui: the Productive Cycle, the Controlling Cycle, and the Weakening Cycle.

Productive Cycle

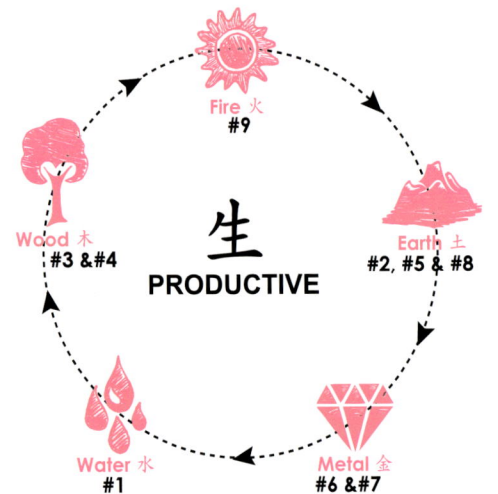

In this cycle,

| Water produces Wood |
| Wood produces Fire |
| Fire produces Earth |
| Earth produces Metal |
| Metal produces Water |

This is a cycle where the elements "produce" one another in terms of providing or helping the growth of another. In the case of Water, then, it produces nourishment for trees and plants (i.e. Wood). An element that produces another element means that it strengthens and grows the element that it produces. Here are some simple metaphors might help you visualize this better:

Water waters soil, producing Wood
Wood makes kindling, producing Fire
Fire makes ashes, producing Earth
Earth is mined, producing Metal
Metal melts, producing Water

Controlling Cycle

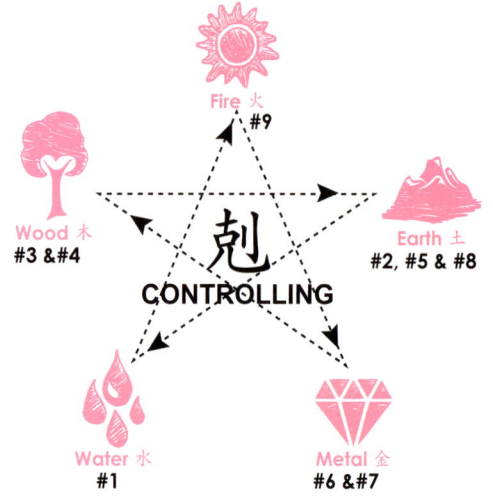

In this cycle,

Fire controls Metal
Metal controls Wood
Wood controls Earth
Earth controls Water
Water controls Fire

This is a cycle where the elements keep each under in "control": an element is countered or subjugated by its controlling element. In this instance, for example, the element of Water controls Fire by putting it out. Here are some simple metaphors to help you visualize it better:

Water extinguishes Fire
Fire melts Metal
Metal cuts Wood
Wood roots tightly grip Earth
Earth contains Water

Weakening Cycle

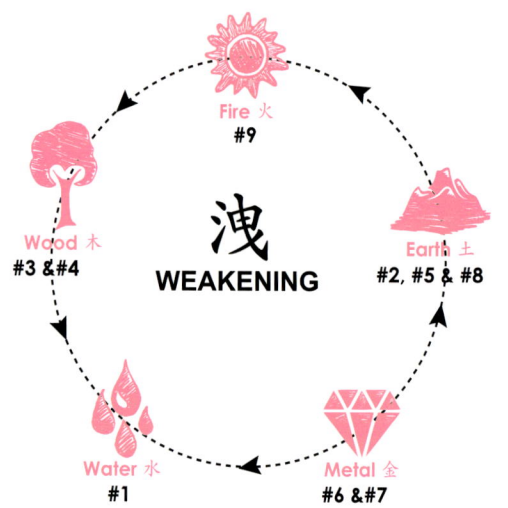

In this cycle,

Water weakens Metal
Metal weakens Earth
Earth weakens Fire
Fire weakens Wood
Wood weakens Water

The Weakening Cycle can be best understood as the reverse of the Productive Cycle, in that the strength of the element is weakened by another in order to keep it in check. Remember, the key to Qi in Feng Shui is balance, and different elements keep other elements from becoming too strong. For example, Wood absorbs Water and therefore weakens it. Again, here are some metaphors for easier visualization:

Water can be partly absorbed by Wood
Wood can be partly burnt by Fire
Fire can be diminished with Earth
Earth is weakened when mined for Metal
Metal is corroded by Water

The following table shows you the Annual Stars for the year 2000 to 2026.

Examine it and figure out where your room lies; in which sector. Take note of the element of that sector and remember that as a Star 8 person, your element is Water.

SE	S	SW
6 White METAL	2 Black EARTH	4 Green WOOD
7 Yellow (E)	5 Red	3 Purple (W)
1 White WATER	9 Jade FIRE	8 White EARTH
NE	N	NW

2002, 2011, 2020

SE	S	SW
5 Yellow EARTH	1 White WATER	3 Jade WOOD
4 Green (E)	6 White	8 White (W)
9 Purple FIRE	2 Black EARTH	7 Red METAL
NE	N	NW

2003, 2012, 2021

SE	S	SW
4 Green WOOD	9 Purple FIRE	2 Black EARTH
3 Jade (E)	5 Yellow	7 Red (W)
8 White EARTH	1 White WATER	6 White METAL
NE	N	NW

2004, 2013, 2022

SE	S	SW
3 Jade WOOD	8 White EARTH	1 White WATER
2 Black (E)	4 Green	6 White (W)
7 Red METAL	9 Purple FIRE	5 Yellow EARTH
NE	N	NW

2005, 2014, 2023

SE	S	SW
2 Black EARTH	7 Red METAL	9 Purple FIRE
1 White (E)	3 Jade	5 Yellow (W)
6 White METAL	8 White EARTH	4 Green WOOD
NE	N	NW

2006, 2015, 2024

SE	S	SW
1 White WATER	6 White METAL	8 White EARTH
9 Purple (E)	2 Black	4 Green (W)
5 Yellow EARTH	7 Red METAL	3 Jade WOOD
NE	N	NW

2007, 2016, 2025

SE	S	SW
9 Purple FIRE	5 Yellow EARTH	7 Red METAL
8 White (E)	1 White	3 Jade (W)
4 Green WOOD	6 White METAL	2 Black EARTH
NE	N	NW

2008, 2017, 2026

SE	S	SW
8 White EARTH	4 Green WOOD	6 White METAL
7 Red (E)	9 Purple	2 Black (W)
3 Jade WOOD	5 Yellow EARTH	1 White WATER
NE	N	NW

2000, 2009, 2018

SE	S	SW
7 Red METAL	3 Jade WOOD	5 Yellow EARTH
6 White (E)	8 White	1 White (W)
2 Black EARTH	4 Green WOOD	9 Purple FIRE
NE	N	NW

2001, 2010, 2019

These Annual Stars shows you the location of the Stars in a property for the duration of the years specified. Based on the year, the Annual Stars will be located in different sectors of the house. Accordingly, different Annual Stars will affect the Feng Shui of your room in different years.

If the Annual Star of your bedroom is of the same element as your Life Star then the outcome is likely to be prosperous (Productive Cycle). If the Annual Star is your Life Star's controlling element (Controlling Cycle), then the result is likely to be stressful – although this combination is still desirable. But if the Annual Star element is the countering element (Countering Cycle) of your Life Star, then the combination is an unfavorable or inauspicious one for you. (Special note: the #5 Yellow Star is generally an undesirable Annual Star for your bedroom regardless of your Life Star.)

Think about the way the element of the Annual Star and your element (Water) interact.

Besides the Annual Stars of the year, there also other factors to be considered. These include the Flying Stars chart of your specific house or property with the Sitting and Facing Stars. Advanced students may want to read *Xuan Kong Flying Stars Feng Shui* for further information. These Stars also affect the evaluation of the impact of the Xuan Kong Flying Stars on your property. There are many other ways of assessing the Feng Shui of a property, and it's important to understand that all these factors play an important and related role.

Characteristics of Star 8

We all have our "good days" and "bad days". Feng Shui seeks to help isolate why this happens and provide advice that you can use to make every day a "good day" where you are in your element. This section outlines the good and bad characteristics of your Life Star. In a positive sector of your house or work, the positive attributes of your Life Star will be further enhanced, and you will display more of these characteristics. In a negative sector, the positive attributes will be diminished and the negative attributes will begin to show through. Your bad characteristics will take center stage.

The Good

Consistent

Out of all the Life Stars, Star 8 people are the most steady and reliable ones of all. Due to your Yang Earth element, you tend to embody the qualities of immovable rock or the ever-present mountain. In your approach to everything, you rarely waver in your standpoint or perspective, and present consistency and sameness in large doses. You don't engage in reckless, impulsive behavior.

Reliable

Because of your ability to be consistent, you do not tire or change your approach once you've got started. This makes you good at seeing things out to the end and getting things done. You are unimpressed when others fail to something because of their tempestuousness or change of mood. Others often rely on you to be responsible when it is needed because you also have a strong sense of justice. While you are not frequently argumentative or contrary, if you see injustice taking place you do speak up.

Versatile

You tend to have a wealth of ideas at the ready; a 'storage' of thoughts and concepts you hold in your head for whenever the occasion calls. This is often an overlooked characteristic of yours that takes others by surprise. Your creativity is often coupled with deep intelligence, so most of the time you are able to juggle more roles and tasks than expected. You do have an adventurous side and you are are more open-minded than people give you credit for. You are always open to new experiences, ideas, and knowledge.

Optimist

As a Star 8 person, you are also quite an optimist. You don't reveal this through your actions and instead it manifests itself in the way you view the world. You automatically expect goodness from the people in it and because you treat the people you meet well, you more often than not tend to receive the same treatment in return, validating your world view. In this sense, you try to see the good in things and situations and people and try to act in ways that are meaningful and considerate of others, because you truly believe that at the end of the day, it will all work out for the best.

壞

The Bad

Unyielding

When your traits are manifested in an unhealthy way, then your constant certainty becomes your Achilles heel, as you may become rigid and unyielding. You are naturally resistant to change, and seek to eliminate anything that may divert you from your usual or planned routine. As such, you may cut yourself from many potentially life-changing things because you can be determined to stick to your original plan. In this case, unreasonable adherence to plans can actually stop you from achieving your goals!

Passive

At your worst, you can fail to take action when it is needed, and expect things to constantly come your way instead. You may be passive and lack the motivation or initiative to get things going, particularly where issues of finance and wealth are concerned. It is one thing to be unwilling to engage in ruthless and competitive pursuits but it is quite another thing to sit back and refuse to take action. Passiveness, if left unchecked, can become something quite dangerous for you in the long run.

Inexpressive

Partly because your emotions and feelings are deep and well-hidden, you may sometimes lose touch with your exact sentiments and be unable to express yourself. This can be a problem in your relationships, as you will be unable to share what you really feel or think, and this prevents others from feeling like they really know you. Furthermore, you may be unable to ask or demand for the right thing if you don't know how to express yourself, and you risk being marginalized or excluded because of this.

Isolated

Despite your optimism, perhaps paradoxically, you may also have a skeptical streak – particularly if all the previous negative traits are in play. While independence is a good thing, being stubborn, inexpressive, and rigid can make you more alone than ever. There is a tendency for you to isolate yourself from company and social interactions as you become more entrenched in your own way of doing things and convince yourself that your way is the only right way!

職業和財富

CAREER AND WEALTH

Characteristics at Work

As a Star 8 person, you may display some of these basic characteristics in professional situations at the workplace and in relation to your career. Being aware of your own key characteristics will help you understand why you act and react to situations, people, and tasks in the way you do.

This section outlines the good and bad characteristics of your Life Star. In a positive sector of your house or work, the positive attributes of your Life Star will be further enhanced, and you will display more of these characteristics. In a negative sector, the positive attributes will be diminished and the negative attributes will begin to show through. Your bad characteristics will take center stage.

• Steady

One of your key strengths when it comes to the workplace is your ability to maintain a clear and steady focus on the road ahead. You tend to get into a job for the long-term, and this makes you an asset to superiors and colleagues, as well as potential employers. You move ahead according to a set plan, taking things step-by-step so as to always be on top of errors. Your methodical approach allows success and failure to be documented and tracked which is essential in larger projects.

• Thoughtful

When it comes to making decisions, you consider all aspects of a situation, problem, or potential task before committing to take any form of action. Your decision making process is thorough. This is precisely why you stick your path after making a decision – it is usually because the path has been decided upon after much intensive thought. You value the time and work of others and dislike taking people's efforts for granted, and colleagues and teammates tend to respect you for it.

• Positive-minded

Your sense of optimism also infuses your work ethics and attitude with goodwill, and thus makes you popular among your workmates. You expect the best from others and refuse to engage in gossip or backstabbing. In

this sense, you take a very balanced, mature approach to work in that you do not allow your emotions (especially bad ones) to influence how you do your job or how you relate to others. What's important to you is maintaining professionalism and staying focused on the goals of your projects and tasks instead of getting side-tracked by negative personal issues.

• Self-reliant

You are usually a very independent worker, and prefer to be left to your own devices and allowed to figure out how to get things done on your own. You can be resourceful and independent and you have a good sense of how best to get things done instead of expecting to be helped or assisted by others. You don't need someone else standing over your shoulder helping show you how to do things.

Suitable Job Roles

• Accountant, financier

Detailed, careful, and thorough – those are some of the qualities needed in accountancy and finance work, and the Star 8 character has them in spades. You are capable of maintaining the steady focus that is required by work of this nature, where attention has to be paid as you comb through documents and figures. A careful, responsible nature is a necessity here and you fit the bill. You may also appreciate the fact that these careers let you make important decisions and set goals in a largely independent manner.

• Management

As a Star 8 person, you will be ideal in jobs that require management skills and practicality. Jobs that emphasis quality control and reform will suit your characteristics because you tend to be the person who is solid in implementing policies and ensuring that things are done accurately and within the proper parameters. You are also good at organizing structures and creating a stable work environment that brings out creativity and ingenuity among everyone involved.

• Educator

As an intellectual of sorts possessing great intelligence, Star 8 people often make the best teachers as they have a lot to teach! You have a warm yet respectable aura that often makes students feel comfortable in your presence. Furthermore, you have the

ability to break down complex ideas into structured, smaller components which you can relay to others. Your consistency and honesty means that you understand your responsibility to your students and make yourselves available to answer their questions.

• Science, research

Your problem solving skills and careful attention to detail mean that you will thrive when working in the fields of science and research. Furthermore, intelligent analysis spurs you on to discover different ideas and methods, and you enjoy the mostly calm atmosphere of independent work. Contrary to expectation, you can be bold in probing new ideas because you're confident in your thinking abilities and the fact that you can discover new things if you set your mind to it.

Career and Wealth Guide

• Say goodbye to organization, once in awhile

While your steadfast adherence to system and structure is admirable and valuable, it can also prevent you from reaching your goals in certain situations. To improve your rate of success in life, learn to become looser and more flexible in your approach, because sometimes chaos and messiness can produce unexpected developments and boost your creativity. You'll be surprised at what can be achieved amidst plenty of things going wrong! Mix things up.

• Be more aggressive

While you may well be held in high regard by others due to your kind and easy-going nature, it's also imperative that you learn to get ahead in the workplace by being more aggressive. This does not necessarily mean that you have to be come cold and uncouth, but simply that you have to stand up for yourself more and defending your own interests and position against those of others. Too often, as a Star 8 person, you swallow your disagreement or anger in order to keep the peace.

• Take the initiative

Far too often, Star 8 people forget to push ahead and take the initiative – whether it's asking for help, asking for a raise, or requesting to be allowed to work on a new and exciting project. Sometimes you tend to see the world through rose-tinted glasses and assume that good things will come to those who wait, but that's not how things work in some dog-eat-dog work environments. Thus, be more open to scheming, planning, and proposing. Stand up and be noticed.

- ## Accept/invite opinions

One good way to ensure that you don't fall into the trap of inflexibility and rigidity is to always keep yourself engaged and alert with colleagues and make an effort to hear other people's opinions and suggestions – particularly if they disagree with you! As such, you prevent yourself from settling into a comfort zone where your ideas and thoughts are unchallenged and thus unable to grow.

• Ask for help

We all run into things that we can't fix or solve ourselves. It can be hard to admit that you need help because you are usually accustomed to being self reliant! Be honest with yourself; could you benefit from a helping hand? The answer is usually yes! In matters of finance and investments, as well, be sure to ask around for ideas and suggestions on how best to grow your money – you may be exposed to new options and interesting ideas that you didn't consider before.

Famous Personalities :

Steve Ballmer,
Ted Turner,
Stefan Persson,
Philip Knight

人際關係

RELATIONSHIPS

Guide for Relationships

As a Star 8 person, you have a complex multi faceted approach to matters of the heart which other people may find paradoxical. This stems from the fact that you are a person with a tremendous amount of depth – while you don't deceive or manipulate or consciously set out to put a performance, you certainly throw others with your behavior! Where love and romance are concerned, you tend to be passionate on the inside while cultivating a realistic and cool and calm persona on the outside. You hide your true feelings because you realize that sometimes giving away your feelings can ruin your mysterious appeal. As such, others find you enigmatic.

Because you're unused to expressing your thoughts and feelings, you tend to keep a lot of your most potent ones buried. As such, when you fall in love you need time before you start to reveal yourself, even while you may feel strongly about the other person deep down inside. You still have an innate need to take things slow and don't like to be pushed into expressing how you feel before you're ready to do so. Before this happens, you are quite happy to woo and be wooed and others find you well groomed and generally attractive.

As far as conflict goes in romance, you generally have a straightforward, honest approach which discourages romantic 'drama'. You also value your independence but sometimes this means that you can also be carried away by distractions or external temptations, which is something you have to guard against.

Typically, a lot of Star 8 women tend to be wary of relationships and many choose to remain single in order not to have to give up their independence.

If you get married, you are someone who will put much thought and care into the matter before doing so – and you do so with the intention of staying married for life. But you will have to work on keeping your love alive by frequently expressing what you feel. Do not take for granted the fact that your partner or spouse knows you care. You love your family and you will always put them first. Even outside of a relationship or marriage, if you remain single, you tend to be the one who still places importance on the elders of the family and you are always committed to ensuring the well being of your family members.

Star 8 in relationships:

Star 8 people are strongly independent and are often not attracted to deep romantic involvements. They are reserved when it comes to expressing their emotions.

健康

HEALTH

Guide for Health

Body parts and organs that are related to Star 8: Spleen, pancreas, stomach, kidney.

The organs and bodily parts that are associated with Star 8 are the spleen, pancreas, stomach, kidneys and to a lesser extent, the liver and bladder. You tend to have a craving for sour, salty, and savory foods, and like to indulge in food that is full of flavor but not necessarily healthy! Be selective about what you eat on a regular basis, or you will have to deal with inflammation of the stomach or frequent bouts of stomach flu. In some cases, you can develop gastrointestinal disease if you do not mend your ways!

On the whole, Star 8 people tend to be somewhat weak in health. Your immune system is often subject to attack. As such, you need to pay attention to your energy levels and your general physical well being, or you will constantly be fending off attacks of cold and flu. You will find that you battle frequent illness from a young age, and hence will have to be even more careful as you grow older by taking proper steps in helping your body become stronger and healthier. You do not benefit from the same health baseline as others do and must be proactive in your attempts to fend off issues.

Beyond this, Star 8 people like you also need to watch out for skin allergies, as well as back pain and inflammation. Hepatitis and gall bladder infections are also something you will have to contend with. Furthermore, you may suffer from blood pressure issues, and stress and anxiety contribute to headaches, and in some severe cases, migraine. Dizziness and vertigo may also be a concern.

Potential health concerns:

Spine or back-related issues, including stiffness

Muscular cramps

Stiffness in the joints

Sinus, runny nose & flu

COMPATIBILITY WITH OTHER LIFE STARS

This section examines your compatibility as a Star 8 person with other people who have the same and different Stars. No person goes through life completely alone. Relationships with others form the bedrock of good career networking. Friendships and relations with loved ones, spouses, partners and family make everything worth while. It is necessary to understand how compatible people with different Stars are to prevent conflict and missed opportunities. Bear in mind that issues of compatibility are not definite or set in stone. There are exceptions to every rule. In addition, **the quality of Feng Shui** in your environment helps dictate whether positive or negative traits in people manifest themselves and thus it weighs in on the quality of your relationships with those people. This section serves as a good guide on your relationships with other people of different Stars.

At a glance, Star 8 people tend to get along well with fellow Earth Stars of their own kind as well as Star 2 people. You will get along with Star 2 and Star 8 people because they have similar interests as well as similar approaches in business and wealth, and hence partnerships will thrive. However, your relations with another Earth element Star, Star 5, will not be productive.

As Metal weakens Earth, long term contact with Stars 6 and 7 will result in some form of loss for you. Business or trading partnerships conducted with these people, for instance, could result in potential financial loss. Similarly, be careful in your relations with people of both Star 3 and Star 4. You will also tend to be on the losing end of these connections if you're not careful. Wealth loss is likely through professional connections, while cheating and betrayal are likely in romantic and personal ones.

Your relations with someone of the Star 9 are likely to be quite good, with the result that a connection with this person may work both as a partnership and a friendship. Similarly, a relationship with a Star 1 individual is likely to produce positive outcomes, especially from a business point of view.

The chart below lists element people or sectors you can utilize to improve your compatibility with other Star people.

	Compatibility with others Stars (Individuals)	Seek help from this element people or use this sector
Star 8	Stars 2, 5 & 8 (Earth Element)	Earth
	Stars 3 & 4 (Wood Element)	Fire
	Stars 6 & 7 (Metal Element)	Water
	Star 9 (Fire Element)	Wood
	Star 1 (Water Element)	Metal

巽 SE Xun	離 S Li	坤 SW Kun
4 Green WOOD	**9** Purple FIRE	**2** Black EARTH
3 Jade WOOD	**5** Yellow EARTH	**7** Red METAL
8 White EARTH	**1** White WATER	**6** White METAL

震 E Zhen — 兌 W Dui — 艮 NE Gen — 坎 N Kan — 乾 NW Qian

The following pages will explain in detail the compatibility factor of a Star 8 person with people of all other nine Stars through the Compatibility Meter. The Compatibility Guides give you tips for managing the relationships in question.

| **8** White | compatibility with | **1** White |

Compatibility Meter

When you and Star 1 person get together, the outcome is likely to be very auspicious. This is because the Star 1 person, being of the Water element, will be countered by your Earth element, which is a good combination for you. They are likely to provide support and plenty of assistance for you that will establish your advantages, be it work or in financial matters. Relationships and friendships are also likely to go over well. Star 1 people have a sincere, genuine need to look out for the interests of others. Everyone else passes you by but these people might just be the ones to take the time needed to get to know you and come to support you. Without them, you are unlikely to ever reach out of your own accord and so these people can be of great value to you. You might find that you can learn from them,

too. They can be quite driven and assertive and these are skills which you could learn to develop. At work, you might find that your different work methodologies clash. You like to stick to a plan but they have a unique way of thinking which makes timely opportunities apparent to them. Because of this, they work best from second to second and a strict plan can deprive them of their ability to think on their feet for a better long term outcome.

Compatibility Guide

When you get together with the Star 1 person, you will have to be fully prepared to accept the support that they offer. Open up... what's the worst that could happen? Being independent and self-reliant, you will have to learn that sometimes caring for others and showing your gratitude means allowing them to help you! Furthermore, they will be more than thrilled when you approach them for guidance and direction, so don't be afraid to.

| 8 White | compatibility with | 2 Black |

Compatibility Meter

When you and a Star 2 person get together, the outcome is an ideal match.

Things will get off to a good start even if you are a bit of an introvert, as the Star 2 person's good listening skills will help the relationship along when the both of you don't know each other that well. They will carefully pick up on the subtle things you give away about yourself and over time a friendship can grow – slowly. This suits them as they are patient, like you. This connection will also be ideal for a business relationship, as Star 2 people will provide you with ideal links and help you to build your network. Your work styles are similar which means that disagreements are less likely to arise; you both favor a slow, careful approach to matters which has been carefully thought out, rather than an approach based on unpredictable opportunities. You will find Star 2 individuals practical and dedicated to

whatever task they have been assigned. They will rarely go around you or do anything other than what you are told and since you normally do not have the authority to reprimand people when they go against your wishes this means that you can enjoy a productive relationship without ever needing to fall back on a skill set you don't necessarily have. Romantically speaking, you may be well suited. They are not impressed by overt displays of affection and while you may harbor romantic sensibilities you are quite practical in your approach!

Compatibility Guide

Put aside your doubts and approach these people humbly. The Star 2 person is likely to go out of his or her way to make you feel comfortable, and when you reciprocate this will set the grounds for mutual warmth. When working together, the danger lies in your similarities. When two people who do things by the book come together, they do things by the book. They don't think outside the box or take risks and it goes without saying that sometimes risks do actually pay off! Neither person will challenge the other and so some opportunities will inevitably pass you both by.

| **8** White | compatibility with | **3** Jade |

Compatibility Meter

When you and a Star 3 person come together, the outcome is hard to call.

On the one hand, you do need to be cautious of relationships formed with Star 3 people, but on the other hand, there is a possibility that a good combination can arise for a casual friendship or business partnership. Star 3 people are famed for being straight-talking and straight-shooting and you keep your cards close to your chest. Because of this, a situation can develop where only their interests are brought out into the open and you become highly submissive. Although you will never sway on your point of view, you will simply be incapable of arguing your point with a Star 3 individual even if it has merit. Consequently, business partnerships that develop are likely to be lopsided and unbalanced. There is some hope if a Star 3 individual is your superior as they will then be

ideally placed to make the bold decisions and then leave you to get things done. As friends, there will always be some distance, and it's generally inadvisable that you go any further and pursue a romantic relationship. Star 3 people seek out strong, sweeping romances – when they are in love, they tell the world about it - and as a reserved person you are unable to provide this for them.

Compatibility Guide

Make an effort to get to know the Star 3 person well before you proceed. To do this, you might have to step out of your comfort zone and directly engage them with questions designed to feel out their stance. If you are as inert as you would like to be then you will never get a good handle on whether or not the person should be allowed closer to you. If you're in business together, or thinking of starting a joint-venture, it will be important to note that you're both on the same page before you proceed, or else potential disaster awaits. Star 3 individuals are always looking for the next thing and when that comes along they may leave you high and dry. As friends, there will always be some distance, and it's generally inadvisable that you go any further and pursue a romantic relationship.

| **8** White | compatibility with | **4** White |

Compatibility Meter

When you and a Star 4 person come together, there are likely to be complications. Your initial social interactions may be fairly unremarkable with no chemistry. They are soft spoken and they are unlikely to make any attempt at bringing you out of your shell. As things develop, you and the Star 4 person are likely to come across some form of friction at some point, particularly in close relationships or friendships. They are prone to changing their mind about key issues and you rarely show your cards. When you combine their evasive behavior with your guarded behavior, no strong ties can have a chance to form. At work, you live by a pre planned strategy, decided upon as a result of much thought. Few people are less suited to working to a strict plan than Star 4 individuals. You lack the confrontational traits needed to

keep them in line so you simply will not be able to control them in the workplace and results may suffer. They can also become complacent and once again, unless you can break your calm aura and push them in the right direction, nothing will change. As such, it might be best to form connections with a Star 4 person on a casual scale, as there will be less chance of misunderstanding and miscommunication if the ties don't become too tight.

Compatibility Guide

The grounds for a fruitful and harmonious relationship with the Star 4 person are to know them well – their principles, values, and beliefs. If these differ from yours, there will be a clash and you are likely to bear the brunt of it. Your personality means that conflict doesn't arise often but it also means that you can become a whipping post. Don't get too close too soon, or rely on them and trust them, before you've spent considerable time with them. Approach any situation which requires you to work together with a certain amount of control. If you are the boss you need to remind them of this if you want them to achieve the goals you've set out for them.

| **8** White | compatibility with | **5** Yellow |

Compatibility Meter

The combination between a Star 8 individual with a Star 5 individual is likely to be problematic. In general, the Earth element in Star 8 is incompatible with that of the Star 5, and it's very unlikely that the meeting of a Star 8 and a Star 5 person will result in auspicious ties. When you first meet, you may be taken aback by how assertive a Star 5 person is. They are ideally suited to leadership positions and becoming involved in them is not beneficial. You will not be equals because whilst you are intelligent and strong of mind with your own opinions, this means nothing if you are unable to vocalize them. Even if you do raise valid points in your dealings with Star 5 people, they are unlikely to take heed, being extremely independent and strong if not proud. In partnerships there is bound

to be betrayal and fraud, and relationships and friendships will be plagued by hurt and misunderstanding. The only person who will be hurt, however, is you. You are too calm to inflict any damage.

Compatibility Guide

With the Star 5 person, you need to be careful that you're not initially taken in or won over by charm or appearances. The combination of a Star 8 and Star 5 person is likely to result only in bitterness and fraud, so if you have to interact with them or build connections of any sort – especially for work – it will be best to keep things fluid and casual and distant. You enjoy working to a plan so you should plan an "escape route" into your dealings so that you do not find yourself having to get too involved with them. They will be very keen to use you to help in their plans but you will receive no benefit from doing so.

| **8** White | compatibility with | **6** White |

Compatibility Meter

When you and Star 6 person get together, the effect is likely to be unfavorable.

The Star 6 person and you are unlikely to find common ground. It will not be impossible, but there will be significant barriers to overcome. Financial and business partnerships are likely to leave you on the losing end, as wealth loss and failure is bound to occur. This is partly because Star 6 people are of the Metal element and Metal weakens Earth over time. Star 6 individuals make excellent leaders and their great strength lies in their ability to delegate and get other people to do things. You are their ideal partner because you will do as you are told without much fuss and you will do it well. The question is, are you happy to simply do their bidding constantly? Although Star 6 people are not manipulative

– quite the opposite as they stand for fairness and justice – you can fall into the trap of being controlled by them at work or in your personal life. Romantically speaking, neither of you will be good at expressing yourselves which can sink your chances of getting involved with one another! One of you will need to break the ice somehow and make the first moves, giving the other time to follow suit.

Compatibility Guide

If you meet a Star 6 person in romantic terms, then there is possibility that you could have a good relationship assuming that both are willing to work hard. You cannot be evasive and avoid problems with the Star 6 person, or retreat into yourself and take comfort in your independence whenever problems arise. You will need to communicate.

| 8 White | compatibility with | 7 Red |

Compatibility Meter

When you get together with a Star 7 person, the result can be detrimental for you. Once again, your placidity does not work in your favor. Star 7 people are outrageously extravagant, loud and lively. Much like your connection to a Star 6 person, any relationship you have with a Star 7 individual will require some conscious work on your behalf. A friendship might be able to work out, if you want it to and if you arc willing to step outside your comfort zone. A Star 7 person can show you how to have fun for once and time spent with them may give you a taste for a life that revolves around people rather than work. Work partnerships based on mutual professional interests will likely backfire, with you bearing the brunt of the fallout and sustaining some losses. Ultimately, it can be said that Star 7 people are very self-centered and they may take a condescending attitude towards you as you are less vocal and assertive. An unhealthy lop sided dynamic can emerge and you will be the one that pays the price when they move onto better things.

Compatibility Guide

It will be important for you to evaluate the Star 7 person's actual motives, particularly if this is a work or business venture that could generate profits. If they are in it for private motives or benefits, you will have to cut your losses and end the partnership early so as not to have the rug pulled out from under your feet later on. Otherwise, you will have a big mess to clean up, particularly if it involves fraud and misused funds.

| **8** White | compatibility with | **8** White |

Compatibility Meter

When Star 8 people get together with Star 8 people, the result is likely to be warm. Your similar personalities will not clash – instead, they will click together like two halves of a circle. As such, this arrangement will work for partnerships and business ventures, as both of you will have similar working styles and similar values and goals for long-term projects. In friendships and relationships, you will see eye-to-eye and endure very little friction. You are ideally suited!

Compatibility Guide

Your relationship with the Star 8 person will be ideal on all fronts, be it in romantic relationships, friendships, or partnerships. The problems will come from the outside, as others jealous or envious of your connection will try to create mischief and drive a wedge between you. As such, don't pay attention to comments from others. If you do, a situation can develop where you listen to outsiders first before first talking to each other. Your poor communication skills can ruin an otherwise ideal connection. In a romance, especially, try to eradicate suspicion and confusion by talking to each other frankly about any issues that come up instead of evading them. Otherwise, you will cause yourself a lot of damage by holding on to painful thoughts. You will come to learn that things are always better out in the open.

| 8 White | compatibility with | 9 Purple |

Compatibility Meter

When you and a Star 9 person come together, the outcome is likely to be good for you. The Star 9 person is able to provide a warm place of shelter for you from the troubles of the world, and as such in friendships and relationships you can seek comfort from their presence. They are naturally attuned to the needs of others and they will be likely to pick up on your distresses even when you are unwilling to make a fuss about them. For professional connections, the Star 9 person is bound to be a good trading and business partner who will not only look out for their own interests, but yours as well. If you can learn to work together as equals – you can let things slide even when you disagree with them – then you may enjoy a complementary dynamic. You are great at fleshing things out in great detail and planning

meticulously whilst Star 9 individuals can bring spontaneous ideas to the table. You will find their example to be inspiring. In a romantic relationship, you might find that Star 9 people are expressive and forward. Don't let this scare you off because the potential for a great partner does lie within them.

Compatibility Guide

While this will generally be a good friendship and/or romantic relationship, you have to be able to manage your emotions well so as to not scare off the Star 9 person. This means owning up to your feelings as and when they occurs, instead of repressing them or trying to avoid them and letting it all come out in a fury later on! Also be aware that Star 9 people are prone to sudden changes of heart so you will have to prepare to expect the unexpected from them. When it comes to business this means that you will probably find yourself keeping them on track and keeping them focused. Make sure that ideas they present to you properly hold water before proceeding.

About Joey Yap

Joey Yap first began learning about Chinese Metaphysics from masters in the field when he was fifteen.

Despite having graduated with a Commerce degree in Accounting, Joey never became an accountant. Instead, he began to give seminars, talks and professional Chinese Metaphysic consultations in Malaysia, Singapore, India, Australia, Canada, England, Germany and the United States, becoming a household name in the field.

By the age of twenty-six, Joey became a self-made millionaire and in 2008, he was listed in The Malaysian Tatler as the Top 300 Most Influential People in Malaysia and Prestige's Top 40 Under 40.

His practical and result-driven take on Feng Shui and BaZi sets him apart from other older, traditional masters and practitioners in the field. He shows people how the ancient teachings can be utilized for tangible REAL world benefits. The success he and his clients enjoy, thanks to his advice, is positive proof that Feng Shui and BaZi Astrology works, whether everyone believes in it or not!

Today, Joey has helped and worked with governments and the wealthiest people in Singapore, Hong Kong, China, Malaysia and Japan. His clients include multinationals, developers, tycoons and royalties. On Bloomberg, he is featured on-air as a regular guest on the subject of Feng Shui annual forecasts. He is retained by twenty-five top Malaysian property developers to help determine suitable candidates to take top management, change their space and Feng Shui mechanism, the way they make decisions, and understand the natural cosmic energies that can influence their decision-making.

Every year he conducts his 'Feng Shui and Astrology' seminar to a crowd of more than 3500 people at the Kuala Lumpur Convention Center. He also takes this annual seminar on a world tour to Frankfurt, San Francisco, New York, Las Vegas, Toronto, Sydney and Singapore.

The Joey Yap Consulting Group is the world's largest and first specialized metaphysics consultation firm. His consultancy, and professional speaking and training engagements with Microsoft, HP, Bloomberg, Citibank, HSBC and many more have seen the benefits of Classical Feng Shui and BaZi find their way into corporate environment and culture. Celebrities, property developers and other large organizations turn to Joey when they need the best.

After years of field-testing and fine-tuning his teachings, he has put together a team in the form of Joey Yap Research International. The objective of this Research Team is to scientifically track and verify the positive impact of Feng Shui and BaZi on subjects and ultimately to assist more people in achieving their life goals.

The Mastery Academy of Chinese Metaphysics which Joey founded teaches thousands of students from all around the world about Classical Feng Shui, Chinese Astrology and Face Reading. Many graduates have gone on to become successful in their own right, becoming sought after consultants, setting up their own consultancy businesses or even becoming educators, passing on Chinese Metaphysics knowledge to others.

Joey has also created the Decision Referential Technology™, offering decision reformation training on how to make better decisions in business and in personal life. He has led his team of highly trained consultants to help clients create more positive change in corporate boardrooms and increase production in their companies, helping people see their business outlook for each year so they may anticipate, plan and execute their strategies successfully.

Joey's work has been featured regularly in various popular global publications and networks like Time, Forbes, the International Herald Tribune and Bloomberg. He has also written columns for The New Straits Times, The Star and The Edge – Malaysia's leading newspapers. He has achieved bestselling author status with over sixty-five books, which have sold more than three million copies to-date.

His success is not limited to matters of Feng Shui and BaZi. Although his success is a product of them, he is also a successful entrepreneur, leading his own companies and property investment portfolio. When not teaching metaphysics or consulting around the world, Joey is a Naruto-fan, avid snowboarder and is crazy for fruits de mer.

Author's personal website :

 www.joeyyap.com

Joey Yap on Facebook:

 www.facebook.com/JoeyYapFB

www.masteryacademy.com | +603 - 2284 8080

MASTERY ACADEMY
OF CHINESE METAPHYSICS
Your **Preferred** Choice to the Art & Science of Classical Chinese Metaphysics Studies

Bringing **innovative** techniques
and **creative** teaching methods
to an ancient study.

Mastery Academy of Chinese Metaphysics was established by Joey Yap to play the role of disseminating this Eastern knowledge to the modern world with the belief that this valuable knowledge should be accessible to anyone, anywhere.

Its goal is to enrich people's lives through accurate, professional teaching and practice of Chinese Metaphysics knowledge globally. It is the first academic institution of its kind in the world to adopt the tradition of Western institutions of higher learning - where students are encourage to explore, question and challenge themselves and to respect different fields and branches of study - with the appreciation and respect of classical ideas and applications that have stood the test of time.

The art and science of Chinese Metaphysics studies – be it Feng Shui, BaZi (Astrology), Mian Xiang (Face Reading), ZeRi (Date Selection) or Yi Jing – is no longer a field shrouded with mystery and superstition. In light of new technology, fresher interpretations and innovative methods as well as modern teaching tools like the Internet, interactive learning, e-learning and distance learning, anyone from virtually any corner of the globe, who is keen to master these disciplines can do so with ease and confidence under the guidance and support of the Academy.

It has indeed proven to be a center of educational excellence for thousands of students from over thirty countries across the world; many of whom have moved on to practice classical Chinese Metaphysics professionally in their home countries.

At the Academy, we believe in enriching people's lives by empowering their destinies through the disciplines of Chinese Metaphysics. Learning is not an option - it's a way of life!

MASTERY ACADEMY
OF CHINESE METAPHYSICS™

MALAYSIA
19-3, The Boulevard, Mid Valley City, 59200 Kuala Lumpur, Malaysia
Tel : +603-2284 8080 | Fax : +603-2284 1218
Email   : info@masteryacademy.com
Website : www.masteryacademy.com

Australia, Austria, Canada, China, Croatia, Cyprus, Czech Republic, Denmark, France, Germany, Greece, Hungary, India, Italy, Kazakhstan, Malaysia, Netherlands (Holland), New Zealand, Philippines, Poland, Russian Federation, Singapore, Slovenia, South Africa, Switzerland, Turkey, U.S.A., Ukraine, United Kingdom

www.masteryacademy.com | +603 - 2284 8080

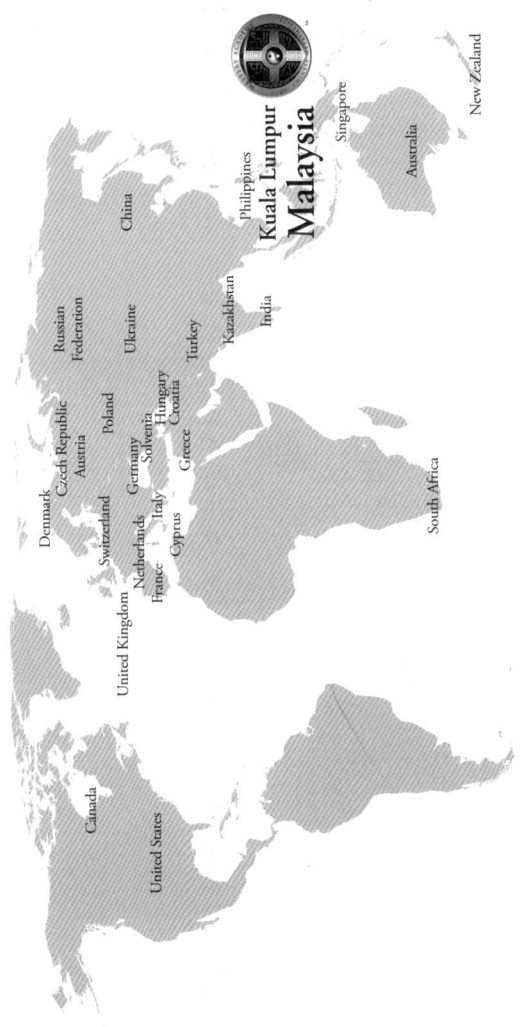

JOEY YAP CONSULTING GROUP

Pioneering Metaphysics - Centric Personal Coaching and Corporate Consulting

The Joey Yap Consulting Group is the world's first specialised metaphysics consultation firm. Founded in 2002 by renown international Feng Shui and BaZi consultant, author and trainer Joey Yap, the Joey Yap Consulting Group is a pioneer in the provision of metaphysics-driven coaching and consultation services for individuals and corporations.

The Group's core consultation practice areas are Feng Shui and BaZi, which are complimented by ancillary services like Date Selection, Face Reading and Yi Jing Divination. The Group's team of highly-trained professional consultants are led by Principal Consultant Joey Yap. The Joey Yap Consulting Group is the firm of choice for corporate captains, entrepreneurs, celebrities and property developers when it comes to Feng Shui and BaZi-related advisory and knowledge.

Across Industries: Our Portfolio of Clients

Our diverse portfolio of both corporate and individual clients from all around the world bears testimony to our experience and capabilities.

Joey Yap Consulting Group is the firm of choice for many of Asia's leading multi-national corporations, listed entities, conglomerates and top-tier property developers when it comes to Feng Shui and corporate BaZi.

Our services also engaged by professionals, prominent business personalities, celebrities, high-profile politicians and people from all walks of life.

JOEY YAP CONSULTING GROUP

Name (Mr./Mrs./Ms.):_____

Contact Details

Tel:_____ Fax:_____

Mobile :_____

E-mail:_____

What Type of Consultation Are You Interested In?
☐ Feng Shui   ☐ BaZi   ☐ Date Selection   ☐ Corporate Events

Please tick if applicable:
☐ Are you a Property Developer looking to engage Joey Yap Consulting Group?

☐ Are you a Property Investor looking for tailor-made packages to suit your investment requirements?

Please attach your name card here.

Thank you for completing this form. Please fax it back to us at:

Malaysia & the rest of the world
Fax : +603-2284 2213   Tel : +603-2284 1213

www.joeyyap.com

Feng Shui Consultations

For Residential Properties
- Initial Land/Property Assessment
- Residential Feng Shui Consultations
- Residential Land Selection
- End-to-End Residential Consultation

For Commercial Properties
- Initial Land/Property Assessment
- Commercial Feng Shui Consultations
- Commercial Land Selection
- End-to-End Commercial Consultation

For Property Developers
- End-to-End Consultation
- Post-Consultation Advisory Services
- Panel Feng Shui Consultant

For Property Investors
- Your Personal Feng Shui Consultant
- Tailor-Made Packages

For Memorial Parks & Burial Sites
- Yin House Feng Shui

BaZi Consultations

Personal Destiny Analysis
- Personal Destiny Analysis for Individuals
- Children's BaZi Analysis
- Family BaZi Analysis

Strategic Analysis for Corporate Organizations
- Corporate BaZi Consultations
- BaZi Analysis for Human Resource Management

Entrepreneurs & Business Owners
- BaZi Analysis for Entrepreneurs

Career Pursuits
- BaZi Career Analysis

Relationships
- Marriage and Compatibility Analysis
- Partnership Analysis

For Everyone
- Annual BaZi Forecast
- Your Personal BaZi Coach

Date Selection Consultations

- **Marriage Date Selection**
- **Caesarean Birth Date Selection**
- **House-Moving Date Selection**
- **Renovation & Groundbreaking Dates**

- **Signing of Contracts**
- **Official Openings**
- **Product Launches**

Corporate Events

Many reputable organizations and instituitions have worked closely with Joey Yap Consulting Group to build a synergistic business relationship by engaging our team of consultants, led by Joey Yap, as speakers at their corporate events.

We tailor our seminars and talks to suit the anticipated or pertinent group of audience. Be it department, subsidiary, your clients or even the entire corporation, we aim to fit your requirements in delivering the intended message(s).

Tel: +603-2284 1213   Email: consultation@joeyyap.com

Chinese Metaphysics Reference Series

The Chinese Metaphysics Reference Series is a collection of reference texts, source material, and educational textbooks to be used as supplementary guides by scholars, students, researchers, teachers and practitioners of Chinese Metaphysics.

These comprehensive and structured books provide fast, easy reference to aid in the study and practice of various Chinese Metaphysics subjects including Feng Shui, BaZi, Yi Jing, Zi Wei, Liu Ren, Ze Ri, Ta Yi, Qi Men and Mian Xiang.

The Chinese Metaphysics Compendium

At over 1,000 pages, the *Chinese Metaphysics Compendium* is a unique one-volume reference book that compiles all the formulas relating to Feng Shui, BaZi (Four Pillars of Destiny), Zi Wei (Purple Star Astrology), Yi Jing (I-Ching), Qi Men (Mystical Doorways), Ze Ri (Date Selection), Mian Xiang (Face Reading) and other sources of Chinese Metaphysics.

It is presented in the form of easy-to-read tables, diagrams and reference charts, all of which are compiled into one handy book. This first-of-its-kind compendium is presented in both English and the original Chinese, so that none of the meanings and contexts of the technical terminologies are lost.

The only essential and comprehensive reference on Chinese Metaphysics, and an absolute must-have for all students, scholars, and practitioners of Chinese Metaphysics.

The Ten Thousand Year Calendar (Pocket Edition)

The Ten Thousand Year Calendar

Dong Gong Date Selection

The Date Selection Compendium

Plum Blossoms Divination Reference Book

San Yuan Dragon Gate Eight Formations Water Method

Xuan Kong Da Gua Ten Thousand Year Calendar

Bazi Hour Pillar Useful Gods - Wood

Bazi Hour Pillar Useful Gods - Fire

Bazi Hour Pillar Useful Gods - Earth

Bazi Hour Pillar Useful Gods - Metal

Bazi Hour Pillar Useful Gods - Water

Xuan Kong Da Gua Structures Reference Book

Xuan Kong Da Gua 64 Gua Transformation Analysis

Bazi Structures and Structural Useful Gods - Wood

Bazi Structures and Structural Useful Gods - Fire

Bazi Structures and Structural Useful Gods - Earth

Bazi Structures and Structural Useful Gods - Metal

Bazi Structures and Structural Useful Gods - Water

Xuan Kong Purple White Script

Earth Study Discern Truth Second Edition

www.masteryacademy.com | +603 - 2284 8080

Joey Yap's BaZi Profiling System

Three Levels of BaZi Profiling (English & Chinese versions)

In BaZi Profiling, there are three levels that reflect three different stages of a person's personal nature and character structure.

Level 1 – The Day Master

The Day Master in a nutshell is the BASIC YOU. The inborn personality. It is your essential character. It answers the basic question "WHO AM I". There are ten basic personality profiles – the TEN Day Masters – each with its unique set of personality traits, likes and dislikes.

Level 2 – The Structure

The Structure is your behavior and attitude – in other words, how you use your personality. It expands on the Day Master (Level 1). The structure reveals your natural tendencies in life – are you more controlling, more of a creator, supporter, thinker or connector? Each of the Ten Day Masters express themselves differently through the FIVE Structures. Why do we do the things we do? Why do we like the things we like? – The answers are in our BaZi STRUCTURE.

Level 3 – The Profile

The Profile reveals your unique abilities and skills, the masks that you consciously and unconsciously "put on" as you approach and navigate the world. Your Profile speaks of your ROLES in life. There are TEN roles – or Ten BaZi Profiles. Everyone plays a different role.

What makes you happy and what does success mean to you is different to somebody else. Your sense of achievement and sense of purpose in life is unique to your Profile. Your Profile will reveal your unique style.

The path of least resistance to your success and wealth can only be accessed once you get into your "flow." Your BaZi Profile reveals how you can get FLOW. It will show you your patterns in work, relationship and social settings. Being AWARE of these patterns is your first step to positive Life Transformation.

www.baziprofiling.com

BaZi Collections

Leading Chinese Astrology Master Trainer Joey Yap makes it easy to learn how to unlock your Destiny through your BaZi with these books. BaZi or Four Pillars of Destiny is an ancient Chinese science which enables individuals to understand their personality, hidden talents and abilities as well as their luck cycle, simply by examining the information contained within their birth data.

Understand and appreciate more about this astoundingly accurate ancient Chinese Metaphysical science with this BaZi Collection.

Feng Shui Collection

Must-Haves for Property Analysis!

For homeowners, those looking to build their own home or even investors who are looking to apply Feng Shui to their homes, these series of books provides valuable information from the classical Feng Shui therioes and applications.

In his trademark straight-to-the-point manner, Joey shares with you the Feng Shui do's and dont's when it comes to finding a property with favorable Feng Shui, which is condusive for home living.

  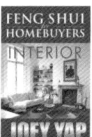  

Stories & Lessons on Feng Shui Series

All in all, this series is a delightful chronicle of Joey's articles, thoughts and vast experience - as a professional Feng Shui consultant and instructor - that have been purposely refined, edited and expanded upon to make for a light-hearted, interesting yet educational read. And with Feng Shui, BaZi, Mian Xiang and Yi Jing all thrown into this one dish, there's something for everyone.

www.masteryacademy.com | +603 - 2284 8080

Continue Your Journey with Joey Yap Books in Feng Shui

Pure Feng Shui
Pure Feng Shui is Joey Yap's debut with an international publisher, CICO Books, and is a refreshing and elegant look at the intricacies of Classical Feng Shui – now compiled in a useful manner for modern-day readers. This book is a comprehensive introduction to all the important precepts and techniques of Feng Shui practice.

Your Aquarium Here
This book is the first in Fengshuilogy Series, a series of matter-in-fact and useful Feng Shui books designed for the person who wants to do a fuss-free Feng Shui.

Xuan Kong Flying Stars
This book is an essential introductory book to the subject of Xuan Kong Fei Xing, a well-known and popular system of Feng Shui. Learn 'tricks of the trade' and 'trade secrets' to enhance and maximize Qi in your home or office.

Walking the Dragons
Compiled in one book for the first time from Joey Yap's Feng Shui Mastery Excursion Series, the book highlights China's extensive, vibrant history with astute observations on the Feng Shui of important sites and places. Learn the landform formations of Yin Houses (tombs and burial places), as well as mountains, temples, castles, and villages.

The Art of Date Selection: Personal Date Selection
With the *Art of Date Selection: Personal Date Selection*, learn simple, practical methods you can employ to select not just good dates, but personalized good dates. Whether it's a personal activity such as a marriage or professional endeavor such as launching a business, signing a contract or even acquiring assets, this book will show you how to pick the good dates and tailor them to suit the activity in question, as well as avoid the negative ones too!

www.masteryacademy.com | +603 - 2284 8080

Face Reading Collection

Discover Face Reding (English & Chinese versions)

This is a comprehensive book on all areas of Face Reading, covering some of the most important facial features, including the forehead, mouth, ears and even philtrum above your lips. This book eill help you analyse not just your Destiny but help you achieve your full potential and achieve life fulfillment.

Joey Yap's Art of Face Reading

The Art of Face Reading is Joey Yap's second effort with CICO Books, and takes a lighter, more practical approach to Face Reading. This book does not so much focus on the individual features as it does on reading the entire face. It is about identifying common personality types and characters.

Easy Guide on Face Reading (English & Chinese versions)

The Face Reading Essentials series of books comprises 5 individual books on the key features of the face – Eyes, Eyebrows, Ears, Nose, and Mouth. Each book provides a detailed illustration and a simple yet descriptive explanation on the individual types of the features.

The books are equally useful and effective for beginners, enthusiasts, and the curious. The series is designed to enable people who are new to Face Reading to make the most of first impressions and learn to apply Face Reading skills to understand the personality and character of friends, family, co-workers, and even business associates.

Annual Releases
2011 Annual Outlook & Tong Shu

| Chinese Astrology for 2011 | Feng Shui for 2011 | Tong Shu Desktop Calendar 2011 | Professional Tong Shu Diary 2011 | Tong Shu Monthly Planner 2011 | Weekly Tong Shu Diary 2011 |

www.masteryacademy.com | +603 - 2284 8080

Educational Tools and Software

Xuan Kong Flying Stars Feng Shui Software
The Essential Application for Enthusiasts and Professionals

The Xuan Kong Flying Stars Feng Shui Software will assist you in the practice of Xuan Kong Feng Shui with minimum fuss and maximum effectiveness. Superimpose the Flying Stars charts over your house plans (or those of your clients) to clearly demarcate the 9 Palaces. Use it to help you create fast and sophisticated chart drawings and presentations, as well as to assist professional practitioners in the report-writing process before presenting the final reports for your clients. Students can use it to practice their Xuan Kong Feng Shui skills and knowledge, and it can even be used by designers and architects!

BaZi Ming Pan Software Version 2.0
Professional Four Pillars Calculator for Destiny Analysis

The BaZi Ming Pan Version 2.0 Professional Four Pillars Calculator for Destiny Analysis is the most technically advanced software of its kind in the world today. It allows even those without any knowledge of BaZi to generate their own BaZi Charts, and provides virtually every detail required to undertake a comprehensive Destiny Analysis.

This Professional Four Pillars Calculator allows you to even undertake a day-to-day analysis of your Destiny. What's more, all BaZi Charts generated by this software are fully printable and configurable! Designed for both enthusiasts and professional practitioners, this state-of-the-art software blends details with simplicity, and is capable of generating 4 different types of BaZi charts: **BaZi Professional Charts, BaZi Annual Analysis Charts, BaZi Pillar Analysis Charts and BaZi Family Relationship Charts.**

Joey Yap Feng Shui Template Set

Directions are the cornerstone of any successful Feng Shui audit or application. The **Joey Yap Feng Shui Template Set** is a set of three templates to simplify the process of taking directions and determining locations and positions, whether it's for a building, a house, or an open area such as a plot of land, all with just a floor plan or area map.

The Set comprises 3 basic templates: The Basic Feng Shui Template, 8 Mansions Feng Shui Template, and the Flying Stars Feng Shui Template.

Mini Feng Shui Compass

The Mini Feng Shui Compass is a self-aligning compass that is not only light at 100gms but also built sturdily to ensure it will be convenient to use anywhere. The rings on the Mini Feng Shui Compass are bi-lingual and incorporate the 24 Mountain Rings that is used in your traditional Luo Pan.

The comprehensive booklet included will guide you in applying the 24 Mountain Directions on your Mini Feng Shui Compass effectively and the 8 Mansions Feng Shui to locate the most auspicious locations within your home, office and surroundings. You can also use the Mini Feng Shui Compass when measuring the direction of your property for the purpose of applying Flying Stars Feng Shui.

www.masteryacademy.com | +603 - 2284 8080

Educational Tools and Software

Xuan Kong Vol.1
An Advanced Feng Shui Home Study Course

Learn the Xuan Kong Flying Star Feng Shui system in just 20 lessons! Joey Yap's specialised notes and course work have been written to enable distance learning without compromising on the breadth or quality of the syllabus. Learn at your own pace with the same material students in a live class would use. The most comprehensive distance learning course on Xuan Kong Flying Star Feng Shui in the market. Xuan Kong Flying Star Vol.1 comes complete with a special binder for all your course notes.

Feng Shui for Period 8 - (DVD)

Don't miss the Feng Shui Event of the next 20 years! Catch Joey Yap LIVE and find out just what Period 8 is all about. This DVD boxed set zips you through the fundamentals of Feng Shui and the impact of this important change in the Feng Shui calendar. Joey's entertaining, conversational style walks you through the key changes that Period 8 will bring and how to tap into Wealth Qi and Good Feng Shui for the next 20 years.

Xuan Kong Flying Stars Beginners Workshop - (DVD)

Take a front row seat in Joey Yap's Xuan Kong Flying Stars workshop with this unique LIVE RECORDING of Joey Yap's Xuan Kong Flying Stars Feng Shui workshop, attended by over 500 people. This DVD program provides an effective and quick introduction of Xuan Kong Feng Shui essentials for those who are just starting out in their study of classical Feng Shui. Learn to plot your own Flying Star chart in just 3 hours. Learn 'trade secret' methods, remedies and cures for Flying Stars Feng Shui. This boxed set contains 3 DVDs and 1 workbook with notes and charts for reference.

BaZi Four Pillars of Destiny Beginners Workshop - (DVD)

Ever wondered what Destiny has in store for you? Or curious to know how you can learn more about your personality and inner talents? BaZi or Four Pillars of Destiny is an ancient Chinese science that enables us to understand a person's hidden talent, inner potential, personality, health and wealth luck from just their birth data. This specially compiled DVD set of Joey Yap's BaZi Beginners Workshop provides a thorough and comprehensive introduction to BaZi. Learn how to read your own chart and understand your own luck cycle. This boxed set contains 3 DVDs and 1 workbook with notes and reference charts.

---

www.masteryacademy.com | +603 - 2284 8080

DVD Series

Joey Yap's Face Reading Revealed DVD Series
Mian Xiang, the Chinese art of Face Reading, is an ancient form of physiognomy and entails the use of the face and facial characteristics to evaluate key aspects of a person's life, luck and destiny. In his Face Reading DVDs series, Joey Yap shows you how the facial features reveal a wealth of information about a person's luck, destiny and personality.

Mian Xiang also tell us the talents, quirks and personality of an individual. Do you know that just by looking at a person's face, you can ascertain his or her health, wealth, relationships and career? Let Joey Yap show you how the 12 Palaces can be utilised to reveal a person's inner talents, characteristics and much more.

Feng Shui for Homebuyers DVD Series
In these DVDs, you will also learn how to identify properties with good Feng Shui features that will help you promote a fulfilling life and achieve your full potential. Discover how to avoid properties with negative Feng Shui that can bring about detrimental effects to your health, wealth and relationships.

Joey will also elaborate on how to fix the various aspects of your home that may have an impact on the Feng Shui of your property and give pointers on how to tap into the positive energies to support your goals.

Discover Feng Shui with Joey Yap: Set of 4 DVDs
Informative and entertaining, classical Feng Shui comes alive in *Discover Feng Shui with Joey Yap!*

You have the questions. Now let Joey personally answer them in this 4-set DVD compilation! Learn how to ensure the viability of your residence or workplace, Feng Shui-wise, without having to convert it into a Chinese antiques' shop. Classical Feng Shui is about harnessing the natural power of your environment to improve quality of life. It's a systematic and subtle metaphysical science.

Walking the Dragons with Joey Yap (The TV Series)
This DVD set features eight episodes, covering various landform Feng Shui analyses and applications from Joey Yap as he and his co-hosts travel through China. It includes case studies of both modern and historical sites with a focus on Yin House (burial places) Feng Shui and the tombs of the Qing Dynasty emperors.

The series was partly filmed on-location in mainland China, and the state of Selangor, Malaysia.

www.masteryacademy.com | +603 - 2284 8080

Home Study Courses

Gain Valuable Knowledge from the Comfort of Your Home

Now, armed with your trusty computer or laptop and Internet access, knowledge of Chinese Metaphysics is just a click away!

3 easy steps to activate your Home Study Course:

Step 1:
Go to the URL as indicated on the Activation Card, and key in your Activation Code

Step 2:
At the Registration page, fill in the details accordingly to enable us to generate your Student Identification (Student ID).

Step 3:
Upon successful registration, you may begin your lessons immediately.

Joey Yap's Feng Shui Mastery HomeStudy Course

Module 1: **Empowering Your Home**
Module 2: **Master Practitioner Program**

Learn how easy it is to harness the power of the environment to promote health, wealth and prosperity in your life. The knowledge and applications of Feng Shui will no more be a mystery but a valuable tool you can master on your own.

Joey Yap's BaZi Mastery HomeStudy Course

Module 1: **Mapping Your Life**
Module 2: **Mastering Your Future**

Discover your path of least resistance to success with insights about your personality and capabilities, and what strengths you can tap on to maximize your potential for success and happiness by mastering BaZi (Chinese Astrology). This course will teach you all the essentials you need to interpret a BaZi chart and more.

Joey Yap's Mian Xiang Mastery HomeStudy Course

Module 1: **Face Reading**
Module 2: **Advanced Face Reading**

A face can reveal so much about a person. Now, you can learn the art and science of Mian Xiang (Chinese Face Reading) to understand a person's character based on his or her facial features with ease and confidence.

Feng Shui Mastery™
LIVE COURSES (MODULES ONE TO FOUR)

The Feng Shui Mastery™ comprises Feng Shui Mastery Modules 1, 2, 3 and 4. It starts off with a foundation program up to the advanced practitioner level. It is a thorough, comprehensive program that covers important theories from various classical Feng Shui systems including Ba Zhai, San Yuan, San He, and Xuan Kong.

Module One: Beginners Course

Module Two: Practitioners Course

Module Three: Advanced Practitioners Course

Module Four: Master Course

BaZi Mastery™
LIVE COURSES (MODULES ONE TO FOUR)

The BaZi Mastery™ consists of BaZi Mastery Modules 1, 2, 3 and 4. In Modules 1 and 2, students will receive a thorough introduction to BaZi, along with an intensive understanding of BaZi principles and the requisite skills to practice it with accuracy and precision. This will prepare them, and serious Feng Shui practitioners, for a more advanced levels and fine-tune their application skills in Modules 3 and 4.

Module One: Intensive Foundation Course

Module Two: Practitioners Course

Module Three: Advanced Practitioners Course

Module Four: Master Course in BaZi

Xuan Kong Mastery™
LIVE COURSES (MODULES ONE TO THREE)
* Advanced Courses For Master Practitioners

The Xuan Kong Mastery™ comprises Xuan Kong Mastery Modules 1, 2A, 2B and 3. It is a sophisticated branch of Feng Shui replete with many techniques and formulae, enabling practitioners to evaluate Feng Shui on a more thorough and in-depth basis. The study of Xuan Kong encompasses numerology, symbology and science of the Ba Gua along with the mathematics of time.

Module One: Advanced Foundation Course

Module Two A: Advanced Xuan Kong Methodologies

Module Two B: Purple White

Module Three: Advanced Xuan Kong Da Gua

www.masteryacademy.com | +603 - 2284 8080

Mian Xiang Mastery™
LIVE COURSES (MODULES ONE AND TWO)

The Mian Xiang Mastery™ comprises of Mian Xiang Mastery Modules 1 and 2 to allow students to learn this ancient art in a thorough, detailed manner. Each module has a carefully-developed syllabus that allows students to get acquainted with the fundamentals of Mian Xiang before moving on to the more intricate theories and principles that will enable them to practice Mian Xiang with greater depth and complexity.

Module One:
Basic Face Reading

Module Two:
Practical Face Reading

Yi Jing Mastery™
LIVE COURSES (MODULES ONE AND TWO)

The Yi Jing Mastery™ comprises Modules 1 and 2. Both Modules aim to give casual and serious Yi Jing enthusiasts a serious insight into one of the most important philosophical treatises in ancient Chinese thought. Yi Jing uses sophisticated formulas and calculations to derive the answers to questions we pose. It is a science of divination, and in our classes there is a heavy emphasis on the scientific aspect of it. It bears no religious or superstitious affiliation.

Module One:
Traditional Yi Jing

Module Two:
Plum Blossom Numerology

Ze Ri Mastery™
LIVE COURSES (MODULES ONE AND TWO)

The ZeRi Mastery™ consists of ZeRi Mastery Modules 1 and 2. This program provides students with a thorough introduction to the art of Date Selection both for Personal and Feng Shui purposes. Our ZeRi Mastery™ aims to provide a thorough and comprehensive program on the art of Date Selection, covering everything from Personal and Feng Shui Date Selection to Xuan Kong Da Gua Date Selection.

Module One:
Personal and Feng Shui Date Selection

Module Two:
Xuan Kong Da Gua Date Selection

www.masteryacademy.com | +603 - 2284 8080

Feng Shui for Life

This is an entry-level five-day course designed for the Feng Shui beginner to learn the application of practical Feng Shui in day-to-day living. Lessons include quick tips on analyzing the BaZi chart, simple Feng Shui solutions for the home, basic Date Selection, useful Face Reading techniques and practical Water formulas. A great introduction course on Chinese Metaphysics studies for beginners.

Joey Yap's
Design Your Destiny

This is a three-day life transformation program designed to inspire awareness and action for you to create a better quality of life. It introduces the DRT™ (Decision Referential Technology) method, which utilizes the BaZi Personality Profiling system to determine the right version of you, and serves as a tool to help you make better decisions and achieve a better life in the least resistant way possible based on your Personality Profile Type.

Walk the Mountains! Learn Feng Shui in a Practical and Hands-on Program

  Feng Shui Mastery Excursion™

Learn landform (Luan Tou) Feng Shui by walking the mountains and chasing the Dragon's vein in China. This Program takes the students in a study tour to examine notable Feng Shui landmarks, mountains, hills, valleys, ancient palaces, famous mansions, houses and tombs in China. The Excursion is a 'practical' hands-on course where students are shown to perform readings using the formulas they've learnt and to recognize and read Feng Shui Landform (Luan Tou) formations.

Read about China Excursion here:
http://www.fengshuiexcursion.com

Mastery Academy courses are conducted around the world. Find out when will Joey Yap be in your area by visiting **www.masteryacademy.com** or call our office at **+603-2284 8080**.